UNDERSTANDING MENTAL DISORDERS

What Is Bipolar Disorder?

Other titles in the *Understanding Mental Disorders* series include:

What Are Sleep Disorders?

What Is Anxiety Disorder?

What Is Panic Disorder?

What Is Schizophrenia?

What Is Self-Injury Disorder?

What Is Bipolar Disorder?

Andrea C. Nakaya

ReferencePoint Press®

San Diego, CA

© 2016 ReferencePoint Press, Inc.
Printed in the United States

For more information, contact:
ReferencePoint Press, Inc.
PO Box 27779
San Diego, CA 92198
www.ReferencePointPress.com

LIBRARY OF CONGRESS CATALOGING-IN-PUBLICATION DATA

Nakaya, Andrea C., 1976-
  What is bipolar disorder? / by Andrea C. Nakaya.
    pages cm. -- (Understanding mental disorders)
  Audience: Grade 9 to 12.
  Includes bibliographical references and index.
  ISBN-13: 978-1-60152-922-0 (hardback)
  ISBN-10: 1-60152-922-8 (hardback)
  1. Manic-depressive illness--Juvenile literature. I. Title.
  RC516.N35 2016
  616.89'5--dc23
                                                    2015009489

CONTENTS

Introduction   6
A Bigger Problem than Most People Realize

Chapter One   10
What Is Bipolar Disorder?

Chapter Two   25
What Causes Bipolar Disorder?

Chapter Three   37
What Is It like to Live with Bipolar Disorder?

Chapter Four   51
Can Bipolar Disorder Be Treated or Cured?

Source Notes   65

Organizations to Contact   70

For Further Research   73

Index   75

Picture Credits   79

About the Author   80

INTRODUCTION

A Bigger Problem than Most People Realize

Demi Lovato is a singer, actress, and former judge on the television show *The X Factor*. But despite enjoying a level of success that many people can only dream about, her life has also been a struggle. In a 2011 article in *People* magazine, Lovato admitted that for much of her life she has battled depression and also struggled to control her actions and emotions. For a long time she did not understand why she felt this way.

Then, when Lovato was eighteen years old, she entered a facility to obtain treatment for an eating disorder and self-harm through cutting. According to news reports, while there she received a surprising diagnosis: bipolar disorder. She finally had an explanation for the intense energy and lack of control she sometimes felt and for the crushing depression she also experienced. Lovato says her diagnosis was actually a relief because she could finally start to understand what was happening to her and how to make her life better. "I feel like I am in control now where my whole life I wasn't in control,"[1] she says. Lovato's struggle is not uncommon. Millions of people in the United States suffer from bipolar disorder, often without realizing it. This illness is a far bigger problem than most people realize.

A Very Common Illness

Research shows that bipolar disorder is one of the most common types of mental illnesses, affecting a significant percentage of the population. Yet even though it is so common, most people suffer for years before they are correctly diagnosed. According to the National Alliance on Mental Illness, every year 2.9 percent of the US population is diagnosed with bipolar disorder. Like Lovato, many of these people

Singer and actress Demi Lovato has enjoyed the exciting life of a celebrity. She has also experienced the struggles of living with the extreme highs and lows of bipolar disorder.

experience years of confusion and frustration before they receive a diagnosis. The Depression and Bipolar Support Alliance reports that people with bipolar disorder can suffer for up to ten years before they receive an accurate diagnosis; only one in four people are correctly diagnosed in less than three years. Study results published in 2011 in the *Archives of General Psychiatry* show a similar lack of treatment: Researchers found that out of more than sixty thousand people in eleven different countries, less than half of those who had symptoms of bipolar disorder had actually received mental health treatment. In low-income countries only about 25 percent had.

One reason many people go so long without treatment is that bipolar disorder can be difficult to diagnose. Even though it is a biological illness, there is no definitive medical test—such as a blood test or a genetic test—to establish whether a person has it. In the United States doctors diagnose bipolar disorder with guidelines from the American Psychiatric Association's *Diagnostic and Statistical Manual of Mental Disorders* (DSM). They collect family histories, interview patients, and review patients' medical history to determine if they have the symptoms of the illness as defined in the DSM. However, since every patient experiences a different combination and intensity of symptoms, even with the DSM guidelines bipolar disorder can be difficult for doctors to identify. Furthermore, some of the symptoms of bipolar disorder are similar to those of other illnesses such as depression, schizophrenia, and attention-deficit/hyperactivity disorder, which makes diagnosis even more challenging.

Physician Robert Grieco is among the many doctors who have overlooked this disorder. When he finally learned to understand bipolar disorder and recognize its symptoms, he reports being surprised at how many of his patients actually suffered from it. "As it turns out, this disorder, which I thought was so rare, is anything but rare," he says. "Every day I had been seeing patients with all of the signs of BD [bipolar disorder], but because of my preconceptions, I did not recognize them. I was not alone in my problem." He stresses that the extent of bipolar disorder in the United States is being underestimated. "It is much more common and much more deadly than we think it is, and does not look like what we think it looks like."[2]

The Need for Recognition and Treatment

When bipolar disorder is left untreated, it can be extremely disruptive and disabling to the lives of patients, their families and caregivers, and society in general. The intense and unpredictable mood changes that result from this disorder often make it very difficult for patients to cope with daily life, and they can struggle to attend school, hold a steady job, or maintain social relationships. Substance abuse and suicide are also common among people with untreated bipolar disorder. According to the World Health Organization, bipolar disorder is such a serious problem that it is ranked as the twelfth-leading cause of disability worldwide. Untreated bipolar disorder usually becomes more severe over time, with patients experiencing longer and more intense mood changes that make it increasingly hard for them to function normally. In contrast, with treatment many patients can greatly reduce their symptoms, and some even spend long periods symptom free.

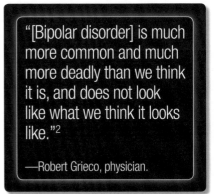

"[Bipolar disorder] is much more common and much more deadly than we think it is, and does not look like what we think it looks like."[2]

—Robert Grieco, physician.

People have no control over whether they will develop bipolar disorder. However, they can take control over how the illness will affect their lives. To do this, though, most need help. In 2014 Lovato spoke at the National Alliance on Mental Illness's "Call to Action" day, where she talked about the need to increase knowledge and reform health care for bipolar disorder and other mental illnesses. "Even with access to so much," she said, "my journey has not been an easy one."[3] As Lovato points out, living with bipolar disorder can be a struggle no matter who a person is. Yet unlike Lovato, many sufferers do not have the knowledge, financial means, or support they need to deal with this illness, which makes their experience even more difficult. By increasing awareness and understanding of bipolar disorder, society can help reduce suffering and improve the quality of life for many people.

CHAPTER 1

What Is Bipolar Disorder?

Bipolar disorder is a mood disorder. It causes shifts in mood and energy that are much more extreme than the normal ups and downs that most people experience. It is a biological condition, meaning that these mood changes are the result of biological processes in the body. Although some people can change their mood by making a strong effort to do so, it is impossible for someone with bipolar disorder to simply will him- or herself into a different mood. Francis Mark Mondimore, a psychiatrist at the Johns Hopkins University School of Medicine, describes it this way:

> Imagine a person whose temperature regulation system doesn't work correctly—a person who suddenly starts shivering on a warm sunny day or breaks out into a sweat in a room in which everyone else is chilly. This person's reactions to warm and cold are abnormal; her body "thinks" it is cold when it isn't and she feels hot when the temperature is cool. We can think of mood disorders as problems with *emotional* temperature regulation.[4]

When a person has bipolar disorder, his or her mood can go from extremely high or irritable—called mania or hypomania—to sad and hopeless—called depression. These mood changes are called episodes. In addition to highs and lows, a person can have mixed episodes, or even stable periods, in between. In most cases, even with treatment the illness lasts for life, and episodes will recur numerous times. In addition, for most people these episodes interfere with their lives at some point, causing them distress or making it difficult to function normally.

Manic Depression

Bipolar disorder was originally called manic-depressive illness. The term was coined in 1896 by German doctor Emil Kraepelin and subsequently used by psychiatrists through most of the twentieth century. In 1980 the American Psychiatric Association renamed the condition bipolar disorder. The new name was intended to highlight the fact that the highs and lows of this illness are polar opposites of one another.

Another reason the illness was renamed was because the term *manic depression* was often associated with psychotic behavior. "People are happier to be labeled bipolar," maintains William Shanahan, medical director at a private hospital in London. "It seems kinder, while manic depression depicts someone running down the road screaming."[5] Some psychiatrists still use the term *manic-depressive disorder* or *manic depression*, though. Bipolar disorder is also sometimes called bipolar mood disorder, bipolar affective disorder, or bipolar spectrum disorder.

Mania

The extreme highs of bipolar disorder are referred to as manic episodes. People experiencing mania often feel extremely energetic and happy. They may also feel creative and full of ideas, with their thoughts racing. It is also very common during mania for people to feel impulsive and take risks without thinking or caring about the consequences. Manic episodes are not always euphoric, though; patients can also feel extremely irritable, impatient, and argumentative. Although manic patients act in ways that are very different from their usual behavior, they often do not recognize that this is the case. Steve Millard, who wrote a book about his experience with bipolar disorder, describes a manic high. "I believed I could do anything," he says. "I seldom slept and when I did, it was never for more than three or four hours. During my waking hours, I was agitated, energized, and virtually consumed with ideas and schemes."[6]

"I was agitated, energized, and virtually consumed with ideas and schemes."[6]

—Steve Millard, author and bipolar patient.

11

Likelihood of Various Manic Symptoms

This chart shows the average rate of occurrence of various manic symptoms in people with bipolar disorder. It reveals that irritability is very common. Hyperactivity and racing thoughts, speech, and ideas are also very common.

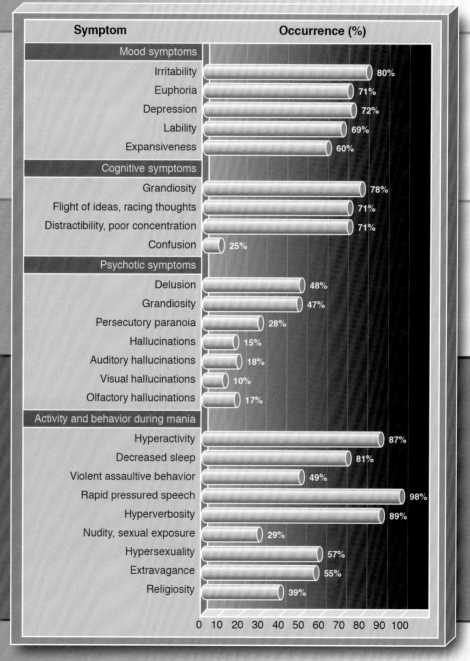

Symptom	Occurrence (%)
Mood symptoms	
Irritability	80%
Euphoria	71%
Depression	72%
Lability	69%
Expansiveness	60%
Cognitive symptoms	
Grandiosity	78%
Flight of ideas, racing thoughts	71%
Distractibility, poor concentration	71%
Confusion	25%
Psychotic symptoms	
Delusion	48%
Grandiosity	47%
Persecutory paranoia	28%
Hallucinations	15%
Auditory hallucinations	18%
Visual hallucinations	10%
Olfactory hallucinations	17%
Activity and behavior during mania	
Hyperactivity	87%
Decreased sleep	81%
Violent assaultive behavior	49%
Rapid pressured speech	98%
Hyperverbosity	89%
Nudity, sexual exposure	29%
Hypersexuality	57%
Extravagance	55%
Religiosity	39%

Source: Eduard Vieta, *Managing Bipolar Disorder in Clinical Practice*. London: Springer, 2013, p. 4.

The DSM has established official guidelines about exactly what constitutes mania. In order to be officially diagnosed with it, a patient must experience a major change in mood and behavior that lasts at least a week, and that change must be severe enough to impair his or her functioning. Some people even require hospitalization when they are manic (in which case their symptoms do not need to last a week in order for them to be classified as manic). In addition to a major mood change, a patient must also have three or more of the following symptoms (or four, if their mood is only irritable):

- inflated self-esteem or grandiosity

- decreased need for sleep (e.g., feels rested after only 3 hours of sleep)

- more talkative than usual or pressure to keep talking

- flight of ideas or subjective experience [personal feeling] that thoughts are racing

- distractibility (i.e., attention too easily drawn to unimportant or irrelevant external stimuli)

- increase in goal-directed activity (either socially, at work or school, or sexually) or psychomotor agitation

- excessive involvement in pleasurable activities that have a high potential for painful consequences (e.g., engaging in unrestrained buying sprees, sexual indiscretions, or foolish business investments)[7]

Although mania can cause people to do and say things they later regret, many people, such as Bryan Timlin, an app and graphic designer with bipolar disorder, find manic episodes extremely pleasurable. "Being bipolar is like jumping out of an airplane knowing you don't have a parachute on," he says. "You know you're going to be hurt, but the high is so euphoric that it's worth the risk. You can deal with the consequences later."[8]

Hypomania

Hypomania is a less severe form of mania. Bipolar experts Trisha Suppes and Ellen B. Dennehy explain, "Those experiencing hypomania feel 'on top of the world,' able to accomplish more than usual, sociable, creative, and invigorated."[9] Suppes and Dennehy say that when people are experiencing hypomania, they frequently say that they feel better than at any other time in their life.

For instance, bipolar patient Tamara says of her periods of hypomania, "Sometimes I absolutely love it. I'm really active and productive. Sometimes I have energy in a way that other people just don't." She says she has received very good grades for the things she has written during periods of hypomania. She insists, "I read them back now and think, 'No way did I write that!' I write poetry and see connections between people and music. I guess sometimes it can actually be a gift."[10] However, just as with mania, during hypomania people often fail to recognize that they are not functioning normally, and they often say or do things they later regret.

Depression

Depression is the opposite of mania. Rather than feeling extremely high, people experiencing depression feel extremely low. When a person has bipolar depression, he or she may be unable to feel pleasure in activities that are usually fun or exciting and may feel extremely slowed down or tired, hopeless, worthless, guilty, or suicidal. Bipolar patient Mike describes how he has felt during periods of bipolar depression. He says, "I didn't want to get out of bed. I didn't want to do anything. I did not want to do *anything*. I didn't want to get up. Breathing was an exercise for me. . . . All I wanted to do was sleep."[11]

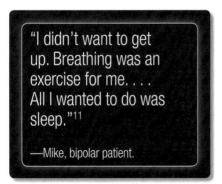

"I didn't want to get up. Breathing was an exercise for me. . . . All I wanted to do was sleep."[11]

—Mike, bipolar patient.

According to the DSM, to be diagnosed with depression, a person must have five or more symptoms from the following list over a two-week period. Symptoms must include one of the first two in the list, a depressed mood, or a loss of interest or pleasure. Like mania, these symptoms should represent a major change from a person's normal mood and impair his or her normal functioning. The symptoms of bipolar depression are:

- Depressed mood most of the day, nearly every day, as indicated by either subjective report (e.g., feels sad or empty) or observation made by others (e.g., appears tearful). Note: In children and adolescents, can be irritable mood.

- Markedly diminished interest or pleasure in all, or almost all, activities most of the day, nearly every day (as indicated by either subjective account or observation made by others).

- Significant weight loss when not dieting or weight gain (e.g., a change of more than 5 percent of body weight in a month), or decrease or increase in appetite nearly every day. Note: In children, consider failure to make expected weight gains.

- Insomnia or hypersomnia nearly every day.

- Psychomotor agitation or retardation nearly every day (observable by others, not merely subjective feelings of restlessness or being slowed down).

- Fatigue or loss of energy nearly every day.

- Feelings of worthlessness or excessive or inappropriate guilt (which may be delusional) nearly every day (not merely self-reproach or guilt about being sick).

- Diminished ability to think or concentrate, or indecisiveness, nearly every day (either by subjective account or as observed by others).

- Recurrent thoughts of death (not just fear of dying), recurrent suicidal ideation without a specific plan, or a suicide attempt or a specific plan for committing suicide.[12]

Just as mania takes over a person's thinking and behavior, so does depression. However, although some people enjoy the manic periods of bipolar disorder, nobody enjoys the depression, because it is

Depression, in a person with bipolar disorder, can make it difficult to take pleasure in activities that are usually fun or exciting. Sometimes it can be hard to just get out of bed.

so overwhelming and debilitating. Grieco describes depression as a huge dip in the road that is covered in fog. He says, "From inside the hole, the fog is so thick that nothing is visible, not even the road ahead. People driving through this depression have no idea how long it will be before they come up on the other side, or whether they will ever come up at all."[13] People with bipolar disorder usually have more depressive than manic episodes, and the depressive episodes usually last longer than the manic.

Mixed Episodes and Rapid Cycling

In addition to manic and depressive episodes, bipolar patients can also have mixed episodes in which there are symptoms of both mania and depression at the same time. For example, a person might have racing thoughts—a symptom of mania—but feel extremely negative—a symptom of depression—at the same time. Having a mixed episode can increase the risk of suicide. This happens when a person feels depressed and suicidal but also has the energy that comes with a manic mood rather than the usual tiredness of depression. This energy makes a person more likely to actually act on his or her suicidal thoughts.

Some people experience rapid-cycling bipolar disorder, which is when there are four or more episodes of depression, mania, or hypomania within a year. According to the National Institute of Mental Health (NIMH), rapid cycling is more common in people who experience a first episode at a younger age and is also more likely to happen in women than men.

According to the Depression and Bipolar Support Alliance, in rapid cycling "mood swings can quickly go from low to high and back again, and occur over periods of a few days and sometimes even hours. The person feels like he or she is on a roller coaster, with mood and energy changes that are out of control and disabling."[14] The alliance says that up to half of people with bipolar disorder experience rapid cycling at some time during the course of their illness. Although rapid-cycling bipolar disorder is extremely disruptive, for most people it is only temporary, and they eventually go back to a pattern of less frequent episodes of the disorder.

Psychosis

People with bipolar disorder can also experience psychosis, in which they lose touch with reality and believe or see things that are not real. This can happen during either manic or depressive episodes. A person experiencing psychosis can have delusions, which are very passionate yet unrealistic beliefs. In some cases delusions are pleasurable; for example a person might believe he or she is a god or has superhero powers. However, delusions can also be negative, such as when a person believes that he or she is being persecuted by the government.

People with psychosis can also experience extreme paranoia, such as believing that aliens are spying on them or trying to kidnap

More than Just Two Poles

The name *bipolar* highlights the fact that people with this disorder experience extreme high and low moods. However, some people believe that this name is not ideal because of the fact that people with bipolar disorder do not just exist at one of two poles, or extremes. In addition to the two poles, there is a huge variation in the types of symptoms people get and how severe they are. For example, some people experience episodes that combine symptoms from both poles, such as depression and hyperactivity. Julie A. Fast, who coaches friends and family members of people with bipolar disorder, argues, "Bi-polar disorder is a bit of a misnomer. Yes, people with the illness do go up and down, but doesn't it seem as if they also go sideways or do little corkscrews as well?" She suggests a different name to better describe the illness. She says, "Maybe if it were called MULTI-polar disorder, people would understand the illness a little bit more."

Quoted in Sarah Owen and Amanda Saunders, *Bipolar Disorder—the Ultimate Guide*. Oxford: Oneworld, 2008, p. 19.

them. They can also hallucinate, which means to see, sense, or hear things that are not really there. Sue suffers from bipolar disorder and has described her experiences with psychosis in the following way: "I quite often think I'm a special person—I'm somewhere between a human and Jesus. I'm better than everyone else, and I have these special insights that nobody else has. Then I start thinking that the devil is trying to get me, and that gets very frightening. And I start thinking that people are working for the devil and they're after me and trying to get me."[15]

Basic Types of Bipolar Disorder

Bipolar disorder is characterized by significant variability in symptoms between patients. All patients with bipolar disorder experience symptoms of mania, hypomania, or depression, but there is a wide variation in exactly how they experience these symptoms. There is also great variation in the amount of time people spend in each type of episode and the frequency of their episodes. Every patient is different. For instance, some people go from high or low mood to periods of feeling normal, whereas other people swing instantly from high to low. For some people an episode lasts for months or years, whereas for other people it lasts for weeks or even days.

Even though symptoms vary widely, doctors classify patients with one of four types of the illness: bipolar I, bipolar II, bipolar disorder not otherwise specified, or cyclothymia. In order to be diagnosed with bipolar I, a person must have had at least one full manic episode in his or her lifetime. Although most people with bipolar I also experience depression, it is not necessary to have had an episode of depression in order to be diagnosed with bipolar I. Bipolar II is diagnosed when a person has experienced at least one episode of depression and one episode of hypomania. Sometimes a person has symptoms of bipolar disorder, but those symptoms do not meet the criteria for bipolar I or II. In such cases doctors classify the illness as bipolar disorder not otherwise specified.

Finally, in addition to bipolar I, bipolar II, and bipolar disorder not otherwise specified, some people have cyclothymia, a more mild form of the illness. In cyclothymia, patients experience periods of hypomania and depression, but their symptoms are not severe enough to meet the definition of a full-blown hypomanic or depressive episode. Because the symptoms of cyclothymia can be relatively mild compared to true bipolar disorder, there is some disagreement over whether cyclothymia is actually a medical disorder. Critics point out that mood changes, including symptoms of hypomania or depression, can be normal and do not necessarily mean that somebody has a medical disorder.

> "Where do you draw the line between moody behavior that's considered 'normal' and the kind of ups and downs that warrant a diagnosis of cyclothymia?"[16]
>
> —Sarah Owen and Amanda Saunders, authors.

Authors Sarah Owen and Amanda Saunders ask, "Where do you draw the line between moody behavior that's considered 'normal' and the kind of ups and downs that warrant a diagnosis of cyclothymia?" They insist, "Even the world's leading experts on mental health can't agree and probably never will. After all, what is normality?"[16]

Prevalence

Bipolar disorder is relatively common in the United States and other nations around the world. The World Health Organization estimates that it affects about 60 million people worldwide. The proportion of people in a particular population who have the illness—known as the prevalence—is typically reported in two different ways. Lifetime prevalence means the proportion that are expected to develop the disorder at some time in their lives, and twelve-month prevalence refers to people who reported that they had symptoms at some point within the twelve months prior to their being interviewed.

A study that was partially funded by the NIMH and published in 2011 in the *Archives of General Psychiatry* provides a good estimate of worldwide prevalence. In the past it has been difficult to compare rates of bipolar disorder in different countries because doctors and researchers often define it differently, but the NIMH study was one of the first to use standardized methodology. Researchers studied more than sixty thousand adults in eleven different countries in the Americas, Europe, and Asia. Overall, they found that the lifetime prevalence for bipolar disorder was about 2.4 percent in the countries studied. Bipolar disorder not otherwise specified was the most common type found. Among all the countries studied, the United States had the highest lifetime prevalence, at 4.4 percent. New Zealand also had a relatively high rate, at 3.9 percent. India had the lowest rate, at 0.1 percent. The rate of bipolar disorder in Japan was also very low, at 0.7 percent.

Statistics from the NIMH show that among serious mental illnesses—illnesses that substantially interfere with people's lives—bipolar disorder is common. The organization reports that in 2012 approximately 9.6 million US adults, or 4.1 percent, had a severe mental illness. In comparison, about 5.7 million people, or 2.6 percent, suffer from bipolar disorder.

Most research shows that bipolar disorder affects all types of people equally, regardless of race, gender, or socioeconomic status. The biggest factor influencing risk seems to be age; people are most likely to be diagnosed with bipolar disorder in their late teens or early adulthood. The NIMH reports that at least half of cases develop before age twenty-five. Although it is possible for bipolar disorder to

Prevalence of Bipolar Disorder

Among US adults aged eighteen or older, an estimated 22.5 percent (or 51.2 million people) were diagnosed with one or more mental disorders in 2012, according to the Mental Health Surveillance Study conducted between 2008 and 2012. Among mood and anxiety disorders, the most common illness is major depression. Bipolar I disorder, according to the report, is much less common.

Past Year Mood Disorders

Bipolar I Disorder	0.4%
Major Depressive Disorder	6.0%
Dysthymic Disorder	1.7%
Major Depressive Episode	6.3%
Manic Episode	0.3%
One or More Mood Disorders	7.4%

Past Year Anxiety Disorders

Posttraumatic Stress Disorder	0.7%
Panic Disorder with and without Agoraphobia	0.9%
Agoraphobia without History of Panic Disorder	0.2%
Social Phobia	1.0%
Specific Phobia	1.6%
Obsessive Compulsive Disorder	0.3%
General Anxiety Disorder	1.8%
One or More Anxiety Disorders	5.7%

Source: Rhonda S. Karg et al., "Past Year Mental Disorders Among Adults in the United States: Results from the 2008–2012 Mental Health Surveillance Study," CBHSQ Data Review, Substance Abuse and Mental HealthServices Administration, October 2014. www.samhsa.gov.

Bipolar Disorder in Toddlers and Preschoolers

Whether children can have bipolar disorder is controversial. However, even more controversial is the issue of bipolar disorder in toddlers and preschoolers. Some therapists, such as Kristen McClure, diagnose very young children with bipolar disorder. McClure describes some of the symptoms of bipolar disorder in toddlers on her website. "Toddlers may appear extremely hyperactive, have difficulty paying attention, act inattentive, or fidgety." In addition, she says, "bipolar toddlers are also easily frustrated and likely to have long drawn out temper tantrums. . . . Often these tantrums are an expression of anger and rage. Parents have described the child as appearing possessed, having a glazed look in their eyes or seeming like a wild animal." Yet critics contend that tantrums, hyperactivity, and emotional upheaval are actually common among young children because their brains are still developing and they are still learning about limits and expressing themselves. For instance, parents often speak about the "terrible twos" because it is so common for children at this age to have tantrums and frequent mood changes.

Kristen McClure, "Bipolar Toddler Symptoms," Kristen-McClure-Therapist.com. www.kristen-mcclure-therapist .com.

develop suddenly in the elderly, this is much less common. Bipolar disorder occurs fairly equally in men and women, though there are often differences in the way it affects each gender. Research shows that it usually begins earlier in men than in women. Women often have more depressive episodes and fewer manic episodes than men, and they are more likely to have bipolar II and rapid-cycling bipolar disorder than men.

Bipolar Disorder in Children

Until the 1990s most people believed that bipolar disorder occurred only in adults. Since then, however, there has been growing recognition of this illness in children, and the number of children diagnosed with bipolar disorder has increased substantially. The Juvenile Bipolar Research Foundation reports that there has been a forty-fold increase in the diagnosis of bipolar disorder in children. The same criteria are used to diagnose bipolar disorder in both adults and children, but because children are at a different developmental stage than adults, the symptoms often look different. Children with bipolar disorder often have more mixed episodes, and their mood swings occur much more quickly, often within days or even hours. According to the NIMH, when bipolar disorder starts during childhood, it is usually more severe.

Although an increasing number of children are being diagnosed with bipolar disorder, there is heated controversy over whether all of them really have the disorder. Critics argue that many bipolar diagnoses are simply cases in which young people and their families are struggling with all the difficulties that can come with childhood and the teenage years, such as mood swings, fluctuating self-esteem, and high levels of energy. Psychologist Enrico Gnaulati argues that one major piece of evidence disproving the existence of bipolar disorder in children is that a very high number of the young people diagnosed with the disorder no longer meet the criteria for it when they become adults. He says, "This flies in the face of the accepted wisdom that the disorder is a lifelong, impairing mental illness."[17]

Yet although critics argue that many cases of childhood bipolar disorder are flawed, there are also numerous stories of young people who insist that their illness is real and that recognition and treatment has helped them enormously. For example, one sixteen-year-old who was diagnosed at age fourteen says, "I had mood swings that were the worst anyone could have ever seen. My poor parents thought I hated them, but really I was sick and didn't even realize it. But now I am on medications for my disorder and I live a pretty normal life."[18]

A Complicated Illness

Bipolar disorder is a complicated illness. Francis Mark Mondimore points out that for hundreds of years, doctors observed patients vacillating between the symptoms of depression and mania, yet it was not until the beginning of the twentieth century that they realized these opposite conditions were part of one illness. "Why did it take more than two thousand years for someone to solve a puzzle having only two pieces?"[19] he asks. His answer is that despite consisting of two primary symptoms—depression and mania—the experience of bipolar disorder varies greatly between different patients. He says, "Bipolar disorder is the chameleon of psychiatric disorders, changing its symptoms from one patient to the next and from one episode of illness to the next even in the same patient."[20] Despite this variation, bipolar patients have one thing in common: They suffer from a serious biological illness that has a significant effect on their lives.

CHAPTER 2

What Causes Bipolar Disorder?

The human brain controls our moods through billions of cells called neurons. What people experience as thoughts and feelings are actually a result of these cells exchanging millions of chemical and electrical signals. It is an incredibly complex system involving numerous chemicals and a very sophisticated nerve structure. This system works well in most people, keeping moods fairly consistent and predictable. In some people, however, the system malfunctions, resulting in the extreme, uncontrollable mood fluctuations that characterize bipolar disorder.

Because this system is so complex, researchers do not even have a complete understanding of how it works in healthy individuals. They have even less understanding about what causes it to malfunction and cause bipolar disorder. Some likely causes have been identified, though there remain many gaps in the understanding of the origins of this complicated disorder.

Genetics

Scientists do know that there is a strong genetic component to bipolar disorder. In fact, of all the possible causes of the disorder, genetics has the strongest support. Numerous research studies have established that bipolar disorder often runs in families. Researchers have found that a child with a parent or sibling who has bipolar disorder is significantly more likely to develop the disorder than somebody who has no family history. For example, in 2012 researchers in the *Journal of Psychiatry & Neuroscience* analyzed numerous studies on bipolar disorder and reported that the risk of a person developing the disorder is about 0.5 to 1 percent in the general population. However, in people who have a first-degree relative with the disorder, the risk is 15 to 30 percent, and in those with two affected first-degree relatives, the risk is up to 75 percent. (A first-degree relative is a person's parent, sibling, or child.)

According to the Depression and Bipolar Support Alliance, more than two-thirds of people with bipolar disorder have at least one close relative with bipolar disorder or depression. As a result of such strong correlations, researchers believe that bipolar disorder is at least partly caused by genes and that people who inherit certain genes from their parents are more likely to get it.

Twin studies also lend strong support to the idea that bipolar disorder is at least partially caused by genetics. In twin studies, researchers study identical twins because they have exactly the same genes. If one twin develops bipolar disorder, researchers investigate whether the other does, too. If both twins develop the disorder, researchers see this as evidence that genetics is a cause. The twin studies that have

Studies involving identical twins strongly suggest that bipolar disorder might have a genetic component. These studies have shown that when one twin has the disorder, the other is 75 percent more likely to develop it.

Antidepressants and Bipolar Disorder

Although some people with bipolar disorder take antidepressants to manage their illness, there is evidence that taking an antidepressant can actually trigger development of the disorder. Researchers believe this happens to people who are already genetically susceptible to developing it. Sometimes a genetically susceptible person becomes depressed and goes to the doctor for treatment. Depression alone does not mean a person has bipolar disorder (he or she must also suffer from an episode of mania or hypomania). After observing the patient's depression, the doctor will usually prescribe an antidepressant. In some people the antidepressant triggers a manic or hypomanic episode. This means that the patient has now suffered from both a manic and depressive episode and officially meets the criteria for bipolar disorder. Because of this risk, the US Food and Drug Administration warns that doctors should screen patients for bipolar disorder before prescribing an antidepressant.

been conducted do show that when one twin has bipolar disorder, the other is significantly more likely to develop it too; up to 75 percent more likely, according to some research.

In addition, some twin studies have involved twins who were adopted and grew up in different households. This is important because some critics argue that twins might both develop bipolar disorder not because of their genes, but because of something else they are both exposed to when they grow up together—for example, a certain parenting style. However, even in those studies in which twins grew up in separate homes, researchers have found that when one twin has the disorder, the other twin has a much higher chance of developing it, too.

Understanding Genetic Risk

Scientists know that illness can be a result of genetics. In fact, they have long understood that many aspects of who a person is or becomes are genetically determined. Every cell in the human body contains twenty-five thousand to thirty-five thousand genes. These genes are made up of information inherited from both a person's parents, and they work like instruction manuals, telling the body how to make and operate all its parts. Genes are thus extremely important in determining how a person thinks and behaves. They are also responsible for determining how the body works and are thus the cause of many types of illnesses.

Because it is clear that genes are a cause of bipolar disorder, researchers are trying to understand exactly what genes make this disorder more likely and how they do so. Genes are extremely complex, though researchers already have a good understanding of how they cause some illnesses. For example, they have discovered that cystic fibrosis—a life-threatening disease that affects the lungs and the digestive system—is caused by defects in the CFTR gene. It is also known that in order to get cystic fibrosis, a person must inherit a defective copy of the gene from both parents. Unlike cystic fibrosis however, the genetic causes of bipolar disorder seem to be more complicated. Scientists do not believe that a single gene is responsible for causing bipolar disorder; they think that many genes interact to cause this illness. They have had an extremely difficult time identifying which genes are involved, though.

Similarity with Other Mental Disorders

Researchers recently made more progress toward understanding the genetic component of bipolar disorder through the Psychiatric Genomics Consortium (PGC). This is an international collaboration in which scientists have shared genetic data on more than one hundred thousand people in order to get a better understanding of various psychiatric disorders, including bipolar disorder. PGC researchers include more than three hundred scientists at eighty research centers in twenty different countries.

In 2013 researchers announced that they had discovered that bipolar disorder seems to have some of the same genetic risk factors as a number of other mental disorders. The researchers compared the genes of people with five major mental illnesses: bipolar disorder, depression, attention-deficit/hyperactivity disorder, schizophrenia, and autism. They found that although these illnesses seem quite different,

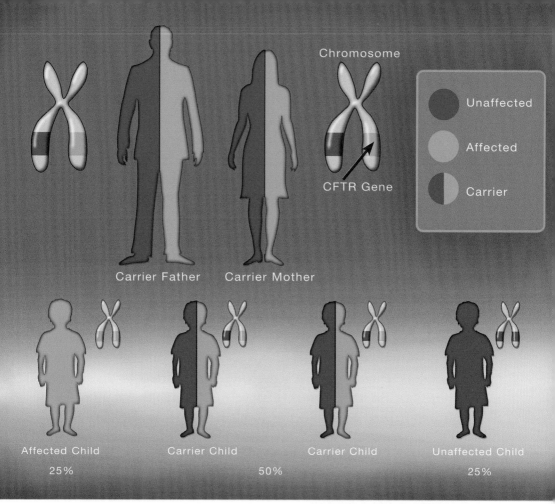

Chromosome

Unaffected

Affected

Carrier

CFTR Gene

Carrier Father   Carrier Mother

Affected Child   Carrier Child   Carrier Child   Unaffected Child
25%   50%   25%

The connection between genes and some illnesses is well known. With cystic fibrosis, for example, inheritance patterns of a defective CFTR gene can help determine the likelihood of a child being born with this illness.

people who suffer from them actually have some of the same genetic variations. As Gina Kolata, a reporter for the *New York Times*, puts it, "The psychiatric illnesses seem very different. . . . Yet they share several genetic glitches that can nudge the brain along a path to mental illness."[21] Researchers believe this is an important step toward understanding the cause of bipolar disorder and coming up with more effective ways to treat it.

Brain Structure and Function

In addition to observing genetic differences, researchers have also observed some difference between the brains of people with bipolar disorder and those without it. A number of studies have used imaging techniques such as computerized tomography scans and magnetic resonance imaging (MRI) to look at people's brains, and some of these have revealed differences in both the structure and function of the brains of bipolar patients. For instance, the NIMH reports that in one study, researchers used MRIs to discover that in adults with bipolar disorder, the prefrontal cortex is often smaller and does not function as well. (The prefrontal cortex is a part of the brain involved in problem solving and decision making.)

There is also evidence that bipolar disorder is related to neurotransmitters, chemicals that help the cells in the brain communicate with each other. Some researchers think that these neurotransmitters do not work properly in people with bipolar disorder. This theory is supported by the fact that many of the medications used to treat bipolar disorder work by affecting neurotransmitters. If a patient's symptoms become less severe by altering the neurotransmitters in their brain with medication, then it makes sense that these neurotransmitters might be involved in causing the problem in the first place.

Overall however, although researchers believe that the brain's structure and function, as well as the neurotransmitters it uses to communicate, might all play a role in the development of bipolar disorder, they still lack a good understanding of exactly how. As neuroscientist William R. Marchand explains, the brain is extremely complicated, and much of it remains a mystery to researchers. "The complexity of the brain makes it very difficult for us to comprehend how it functions," he says. "In fact, some have called the human brain the most complex structure in the universe."[22]

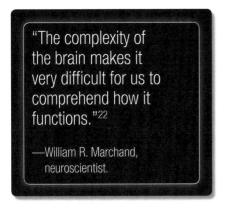

"The complexity of the brain makes it very difficult for us to comprehend how it functions."[22]

—William R. Marchand, neuroscientist.

Environment

Although genes and biology clearly play a role in causing bipolar disorder, it is also clear that other factors are involved. The American Academy of Child & Adolescent Psychiatry (AACAP) points out that although family studies prove that genetics are a cause, they also prove that genetics are not the only cause. The academy explains, "If the condition were caused entirely by genes, we'd expect all identical twins of people with bipolar disorder to develop the illness."[23] However, this is not the case. In many pairs of twins, one develops the disorder and the other does not. Likewise, family studies show that although first-degree relatives of people with bipolar disorder are far more likely to develop it themselves, many do not. This means that something in addition to genes causes this illness. The AACAP argues, "The fact that . . . [not all identical twins develop bipolar disorder] demonstrates the existence and importance of other biological, social and/or emotional variables which can either precipitate bipolar disorder or serve as protective factors in people who are genetically 'at risk' or predisposed."[24]

In addition to genetics, a person's environment plays a large role in the development of many of the traits and characteristics he or she ends up with. Genes are a blueprint for how a person is supposed to develop, but the environment interacts with genes to determine the way he or she actually turns out. Researchers believe this is what happens with bipolar disorder. They think that a person can be genetically predisposed to develop the illness but that in some cases it is certain environmental factors that actually trigger the disorder to develop. In contrast, if these influences are not present, then a person might never develop it, even if he or she has a genetic predisposition to do so.

Specific Environmental Influences

Researchers have identified some of the environmental factors that seem to trigger the onset of bipolar disorder. One is stress. There is evidence that extremely stressful experiences, both positive and negative, can trigger the first bipolar episode. Examples of stressful experiences include starting a new job, getting married, having a baby, or experiencing the death of a friend or loved one.

Experts also believe that a person's ability to cope with stress plays a role. For instance, bipolar disorder might be more likely to develop in a person who has difficulty handling stress and becomes overwhelmed by it. In contrast, a person who can deal well with very stressful situations might be less susceptible to developing bipolar disorder after extreme stress. Other environmental factors associated with the start of bipolar disorder are chronic lack of sleep and long periods of alcohol or substance abuse.

For many young people, leaving home and going away to college can cause the confluence of stress, lack of sleep, and alcohol or drug use that make it more likely for a person with a genetic predisposition to develop bipolar disorder. Russell Federman, director of Counseling and Psychological Services at the University of Virginia student health center, says, "You need a genetic vulnerability for bipolar disorder to emerge. But if you've got that vulnerability, the lifestyle irregularities of the first and second year of college can certainly be a precipitant."[25]

These irregularities can include stress over making new friends and living away from home for the first time, pressure to study hard and succeed academically, and excessive partying. James, a student at the University of Tennessee in Knoxville, says that he experienced his first manic episode after smoking a lot of marijuana and using other drugs, including hallucinogenic mushrooms. "I thought I was having an existential breakthrough, but it was really a manic high,"[26] James says.

Going away to college can add to normal life stresses and result in poor sleep habits and alcohol or drug use. This mix can trigger development of bipolar disorder in a person who is genetically predisposed toward this condition.

Abuse

There is also evidence that an extremely traumatic experience can trigger the development of bipolar disorder. Examples of traumatic experiences are physical, emotional, or sexual abuse. At the 14th International Congress on Schizophrenia Research in 2013, researchers announced the results of a study that showed a connection between emotional abuse and bipolar disorder. They found that children who had experienced emotional abuse were more than twice as likely to develop bipolar disorder. They also found a relationship between abuse and the severity of the illness; more severe abuse was associated with more suicide attempts, a younger age of onset, and more rapid cycling.

In another study reported in the *Clinical Psychology Review* in 2013, researchers reviewed twenty different studies on childhood sexual abuse and bipolar disorder. Overall, the studies included 3,407 adults and youth in ten different countries. The researchers found a strong link between sexual abuse and bipolar disorder, reporting that 24 percent of those with bipolar disorder had suffered childhood sexual abuse.

> "You need a genetic vulnerability for bipolar disorder to emerge. But if you've got that vulnerability, the lifestyle irregularities of the first and second year of college can certainly be a precipitant."[25]
>
> —Russell Federman, director of Counseling and Psychological Services at the University of Virginia student health center.

Head Injuries

In some cases bipolar disorder develops following a head injury. It is thought that in such cases, the injury somehow harms an area of the brain involved in regulating mood. One sufferer, Michelle, believes that a head trauma caused her to develop bipolar disorder. She used to be a very happy person who hardly ever felt depressed or anxious, but this changed after she fell and hit her head.

One snowy day, Michelle was rushing into her office building and slipped on a wet patch of tile, hitting her head hard on the floor. According to Michelle, her head hurt intensely and she felt dazed and confused. She was given twelve stiches and diagnosed with a severe concussion, and she spent four days in bed. "My head pounded and I was just so tired and felt like I was pinned down to the bed. The ringing in my ears was terribly irritating and I could barely focus on anything. Even when I returned to work on day 5 I still felt terrible and very confused. My thoughts were cloudy and I had a really hard time concentrating." She believes this accident may have caused her to develop bipolar disorder. She explains, "Thinking back now I remember a friend of mine that was also a co-worker mentioned to me that I didn't seem myself lately. That I hardly smiled anymore and that I seemed to be short tempered lately. I hadn't noticed and dismissed it. Now looking back I can't help but think that my bipolar disorder started after the fall."[27]

Research also supports the link between head injuries and the development of bipolar disorder. For instance, one study regarding head injuries and bipolar disorder was reported in 2014 in the *American Journal of Psychiatry*. Researchers studied 113,906 people who had been hospitalized for head injuries. They found that people who had been hospitalized with a head injury were 28 percent more likely to be diagnosed with bipolar disorder.

Hormonal Changes

There is also evidence that hormonal changes can cause bipolar disorder to develop. For example, some research has been conducted on bipolar disorder and childbirth, which is a period of great hormonal change. Medical professionals have observed that it is common for women to experience a variety of different types of mood disturbances following childbirth. For example, many women experience postpartum depression (commonly referred to as the "baby blues"), in which they have mood swings or feel depressed for a few weeks after giving birth.

Doctors think such mood disturbances are a result of the significant hormonal changes that occur when a woman gives birth. Most of these disturbances are temporary and relatively mild, though some are more severe. Research shows there are cases of women who develop bipolar disorder following childbirth. In 2013 researchers reported on a study of 146 women in the journal *Bipolar Disorders*. They found that a significant percentage of women who had merely suffered from

Substance Abuse and Bipolar Disorder: Cause or Effect?

A significant percentage of people with bipolar disorder also abuse alcohol and drugs. Some researchers estimate that as many as 60 percent of bipolar patients suffer from substance abuse as well. The reason for this link is unclear. Researchers have found that some people abuse alcohol and drugs in an effort to treat their bipolar symptoms. However, there is also evidence that substance abuse can cause symptoms to develop. For instance, there have been cases in which people develop bipolar disorder following a period of substance abuse. Some researchers believe that for people who are genetically vulnerable to developing bipolar disorder but have not yet done so, substance abuse can cause the illness to develop. Others argue that the symptoms of bipolar disorder are what drive people to substance abuse. Currently, there continues to be disagreement over the nature of the link between bipolar disorder and substance abuse.

depression prior to giving birth developed bipolar disorder within six months of having a baby. Lead researcher Verinder Sharma insists, "Childbirth is perhaps the most important and most potent trigger of bipolar disorder."[28]

Reducing the Risk

Although people ultimately cannot control whether they will develop bipolar disorder, they may be able to decrease their chances by avoiding some of the risk factors that they can control, such as stress or drug use. Bipolar disorder expert Nick Craddock likens this to the way a fair-skinned person can reduce the chance of getting a sunburn. Some people's genetics make them fair skinned and vulnerable to sunburn, but they can greatly reduce the chance of getting burned by using sunscreen, wearing a hat and protective clothing, and staying in the shade. People with a genetic vulnerability to bipolar disorder can take similar measures to reduce their risk. Craddock explains, "You can be born with a higher genetic leaning towards bipolarity, but if you protect yourself (generally making wise lifestyle choices), then you're far less likely to become unwell." He adds that even people who don't have a high genetic risk can protect themselves this way. He warns, "If you're born with a low genetic risk yet don't protect yourself, you may become unwell with bipolar symptoms."[29]

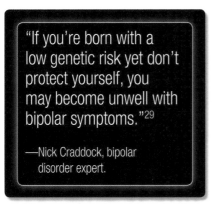

"If you're born with a low genetic risk yet don't protect yourself, you may become unwell with bipolar symptoms."[29]

—Nick Craddock, bipolar disorder expert.

Overall, current knowledge about the causes of bipolar disorder is still limited, and additional research is needed. Researchers know that both genes and the environment play a role, though they do not understand exactly how these factors interact to determine whether this disorder develops. A better understanding of bipolar disorder's causes could significantly improve the lives of sufferers by helping doctors more accurately diagnose patients and provide more effective treatments. Ultimately, doctors could possibly prevent people from developing bipolar disorder in the first place.

CHAPTER 3

What Is It like to Live with Bipolar Disorder?

Peter Goodman suffers from bipolar disorder, and sometimes it is all he thinks about. For example, he writes about how being bipolar changes the simple experience of going out to lunch. He says, "I often wonder if the guy sitting next to me at the lunch counter in my favorite diner has any idea of what I have to do and tolerate just to function enough to sit here with him." Goodman imagines his neighbor at the counter is probably just thinking about his plans for the weekend, whereas the thoughts in Goodman's head are far more complicated:

> I'm sitting there worried about the fact that I am starting to feel jumpy and depressed at the same time, called a 'mixed state,' from which I often suffer. I want to take my medication then, even if it's a little too early. However, I know it makes me nauseated so maybe I should eat first because I probably won't want food for the rest of the day after taking it. I think . . . "My mouth is so dry I can't wait until the waitress brings me my iced tea. Does anyone notice my hand shaking as I pick up the menu?"[30]

As Goodman's story illustrates, bipolar disorder changes a person's whole life. Bipolar expert Eduard Vieta notes that even when people with bipolar disorder receive optimal treatment, they still spend about half of their time experiencing symptoms. In addition to symptoms from the disorder itself, bipolar medications often have significant side effects, as Goodman stresses. For these reasons and more, it is very challenging for most people to live with bipolar disorder.

The Challenge of Being Diagnosed

One of the biggest challenges for many sufferers of bipolar disorder is actually realizing that they have the disorder. Diagnosis is the first step toward understanding how to manage bipolar disorder, though research shows it takes many patients years to be correctly diagnosed. According to Mental Illness Policy Org., an organization that provides information and research about serious mental health problems, it takes most people more than eight years and three to four doctors before they receive a correct diagnosis. In one large survey of six hundred patients with bipolar disorder reported in the *Journal of Clinical Psychiatry* in 2003, researchers found that 69 percent of patients were initially misdiagnosed. A third of patients waited ten years or more to be accurately diagnosed.

Coexisting Health Conditions

Many people who suffer from bipolar disorder not only have to deal with the symptoms of that illness but with the symptoms of other illnesses, too. Experts do not yet understand why, but they have found it is very common for bipolar disorder to occur in combination with other disorders or health conditions. In a 2011 study of more than sixty thousand people in eleven different countries published in the *Archives of General Psychiatry*, researchers found that about three-quarters of those with symptoms of bipolar disorder also had at least one other disorder. Anxiety disorders and behavior disorders were common. According to Vieta, it is actually rare to find a person with bipolar disorder who does *not* have another mental health disorder.

In addition to mental health disorders, the NIMH reports that people who have bipolar disorder have a higher risk of developing a number of other serious health problems, including diabetes, obesity, heart disease, migraines, and thyroid disease. Some of these problems are the result of the medications used to treat the disorder. For instance, lithium is a common and effective medication, but it can damage the thyroid and kidneys.

Substance Abuse

People with bipolar disorder are also more likely to suffer from substance abuse, even though this worsens their illness. The AACAP reports that up to 60 percent of people with bipolar disorder abuse alcohol or drugs at some point during the course of their illness. Researchers are not sure why this is so. One reason appears to be that episodes of mania cause people to lose their inhibitions and make them likely to abuse drugs or alcohol. Another reason is that people sometimes abuse these substances in an effort to drown out their emotions or calm themselves down.

Bipolar disorder is associated with a heightened risk of substance abuse. Researchers are not certain why this is so, although one explanation might be found in the need to find ways to calm strong emotions.

Sleep Disturbances

People with bipolar disorder usually have sleep problems. During episodes of depression, many patients experience insomnia and are unable to sleep, or they feel like they want to sleep all the time. During mania, patients have so much energy that they feel like they need very little sleep or none at all. Physician Robert Grieco says, "I ask [patients] when the last time was they stayed up all night. I am surprised at how often I get the answer 'yesterday,' or 'last week.'" Even if manic patients want to sleep, they often find it impossible. Grieco says that when he asks patients what happens if they lie down to try and sleep, "I usually get comments like, 'My mind is going in every direction,' or 'I wish I had a button on my forehead to turn it off.'" Sleep disturbances make life even more difficult for bipolar patients. Sleep is extremely important to a person's health, and research shows that not sleeping well can have many harmful impacts on mental well-being, cognitive function, and overall health.

Robert Grieco and Laura Edwards, *The Other Depression: Bipolar Disorder*. New York: Routledge, 2010, p. 21.

Psychiatrist Francis Mark Mondimore describes the case of Brad to illustrate how the mood changes that occur in bipolar disorder can cause people to use substances they otherwise would not, such as cocaine. As Brad put it, "I'm not a particularly brave person, and certainly not a fool. But I was . . . I don't know quite how to put it . . . uninhibited, confident. I found myself walking down streets at midnight that I would have been nervous walking down in broad daylight. I bought the stuff and had no qualms about using it. And I was hooked in no time at all."[31] Unfortunately for those who try to manage their illness in this way, drugs and alcohol actually worsen the symptoms of bipolar disorder.

Social Stigma

In addition to dealing with the physical symptoms of bipolar disorder, patients must also contend with other people's reactions to them. Mental illness is largely misunderstood and often stigmatized by society. Like illnesses such as cancer, bipolar disorder is a biological condition that is beyond a person's control, but many people do not understand this. Rather, they incorrectly see it as a personal weakness and something to be embarrassed about. Sarah Owen and Amanda Saunders both have family with bipolar disorder, and they express frustration at the way shame is often associated with the illness. "There's no shame in breaking a leg or being diagnosed with asthma," they argue. "Why the shame of bipolar?"[32] They insist that such treatment is illogical and unfair.

Despite this fact, many people with bipolar disorder face significant prejudice. As a result, patients often work hard to keep their illness a secret. CJ Laymon (not her real name) talks about how difficult it is to struggle with both bipolar disorder and the challenge of keeping her condition a secret. "My illness is a huge part of my daily life," she says. "Just shopping for the perfect mix of medications is a full time job, with side effects from drugs tried and failed ranging from the merely awkward (flushed cheeks) to annoying (dry mouth) to incapacitating (flu-like symptoms that last for weeks)." To keep her illness a secret, Laymon says she sneaks to the bathroom to take her medication when at work and has scheduled phone therapy sessions for as early as 6:00 a.m. so as not to interfere with her job. "I'm still scared of people treating me differently and of my boss feeling like I'm less capable of doing my job," she says. "I want to be the person that uses my real name and admits what I'm going through to put a face to the stigma of mental illness in the workplace, but I can't. It terrifies me."[33]

> "My illness is a huge part of my daily life."[33]
>
> —CJ Laymon, bipolar patient.

Impact on Relationships

People with bipolar disorder often experience unpredictable and dramatic changes in their moods and behavior. These fluctuations can be difficult for other people to understand and deal with. As a result, relationships are often very difficult for patients and for their friends and family. Research shows that bipolar sufferers are much more likely to have marital problems or to divorce than others. Lorna Evans says that her father had bipolar disorder, and it ruined her childhood.

After her mother died when she was only twelve, Evans's father failed to buy her food. She remembers that instead, he spent his days hiding in a cocoon of pillows and blankets and smoking cigarettes. According to Evans, "The day came when I needed to do something. I needed to eat. I went to the doorway of his room and asked him if he was ever going to come out and do some grocery shopping. . . . It stank of stale cigarette smoke. A solid mass of stink. Still no response, except for the sound of another Export A cigarette being drawn from its package and a Zippo Air Force lighter being flicked open. More smoke rose from within his fort. A shotgun poked its nose out."[34] She says that after eating everything in the cupboards, she was forced to ask friends at school to share their lunches with her, and she did so for at least a month.

The impact of bipolar disorder on friends and family can be so significant that it can even cause them to suffer serious health problems. For instance, according to Igor Galynker and Jessica Briggs of the Family Center for Bipolar in New York, family members and caregivers of people with bipolar disorder have high rates of psychiatric problems such as depression and anxiety, and some even suffer from bipolar disorder themselves. In addition, Galynker and Briggs point out that these family members and caregivers are usually so busy caring for the person with bipolar disorder that they often overlook their own needs. They argue, "Family members of patients with bipolar disorder are often 'hidden patients.'"[35]

"Family members of patients with bipolar disorder are often 'hidden patients.'"[35]

—Igor Galynker and Jessica Briggs, bipolar experts at the Family Center for Bipolar in New York.

Impact on Work and School

Having bipolar disorder does not make a person less intelligent. In fact, some people with bipolar disorder are more creative and intelligent than average. However, bipolar disorder can make it difficult for people to function properly at work or in school, because the disorder sometimes causes them to think and act so differently from others. After conducting interviews with young adults who suffer from bipolar disorder for her master's thesis, Regina Elizabeth Bates reported that symptoms of the illness caused trouble for most of them in school. Many said they were labeled as having a learning disability or difficulty. For example, one participant said it took him longer to grasp topics and learn things (although once he did, he said he ended up learning it better than most of the class). Another reported that she sometimes had so many things going through her head that she was unable to take notes.

For adults, symptoms of the disease or of the medications used to treat it can interfere with their work. Some adults, like Evans's father, are unable to hold a steady job because their symptoms are so overwhelming. Others simply have to work harder to manage their symptoms and make time for medical appointments. Blogger Natasha Tracy explains, "Many people with bipolar disorder hold down jobs, just like everyone else. . . . But people with bipolar disorder or another mental illness have special challenges when it comes to work. We're sick more often, we need time off for medical appointments and stress affects us more than your average person."[36]

Financial Impact

Even for people who are able to work successfully, bipolar disorder can cause serious financial problems. This is because during episodes of mania or hypomania, people with bipolar disorder often make impulsive decisions and engage in risky behavior. Such behavior can include spending large amounts of money without thinking of the consequences. Sarah Freeman is one sufferer who says bipolar disorder has ruined her finances. Explaining how easy it is to spend all of one's savings during a period of mania, she says, "Spending in this state is like simultaneously winning $1 billion in the lottery and having only six months to live. Not only does money appear limitless but it seems there will never be any day of reckoning."[37]

In her case Freeman says that she spent extravagant amounts of money on clothing, furniture, luxury hotels, and travel, and she pursued business and personal schemes that she later realized were

During manic episodes, people with bipolar disorder often make impulsive decisions and engage in risky behavior. One woman described how she spent large amounts of money on luxury hotels and travel while in the grasp of a manic episode.

irrational. As a result of her behavior, at age fifty-one she is left living from paycheck to paycheck, with very little savings for her retirement—despite the fact that at one time she was financially successful and had substantial savings.

In addition to sometimes devastating individuals' finances, bipolar disorder is financially costly for the United States as a whole. Treatment costs are estimated to total billions of dollars every year. In addition, the US economy experiences lower productivity overall because bipolar disorder often impairs people's ability to work. The National Alliance on Mental Illness reports that according to research, the average lifetime cost of bipolar disorder per case ranges from about $11,000 to more than $600,000 for people who have many severe episodes or are unresponsive to treatment. The alliance concludes, "Bipolar disorder is the most expensive mental health care diagnosis."[38]

A Productive and Enjoyable High

Although discussions about bipolar disorder are often dominated by complaints about the negative symptoms and feelings it causes, episodes of bipolar mania or hypomania can actually be very pleasurable. During these episodes, patients often feel creative, fun, and energetic. Even their friends agree that they can be fun to be with during these times. Bipolar patient Paul explains, "Unless you've experienced a hypomanic phase, you can't possibly know how wonderful bipolar can be. That feeling does almost make it worthwhile. It's such a good feeling. No narcotic would give you that kind of feeling."[39]

In addition to simply making a person feel good, a manic or hypomanic high can also enhance creativity. A significant number of famous writers, artists, and other creative people have said that their best creative outbursts occurred during such episodes. For example, British television writer Paul Abbott says that when he was sixteen years old he surprised his family and himself by winning a writing competition with something he wrote during a manic phase. He insists that before winning that competition nobody—including himself—knew that he was interested in writing or even good at it. According to Abbott, it is during his life's various manic phases that he has been a very prolific and talented writer and won numerous prizes. "During my last manic cyclone, I created and produced not one but two full primetime drama series . . . in a 12-month period."[40]

> "Unless you've experienced a hypomanic phase, you can't possibly know how wonderful bipolar can be."[39]
>
> —Paul, bipolar patient.

Some research shows that people with bipolar disorder are more likely than people without it to have creative occupations. For example, in a study published in 2012 in the *Journal of Psychiatric Research*, researchers reported that their analysis of more than 1 million Swedish people showed an association between creative professions and bipolar disorder. For instance, they found that authors suffered from bipolar disorder more than twice as often as people without it did.

Bipolar Disorder and Celebrity

Because of bipolar disorder's link to creativity, it is perhaps not surprising that many artists, actors, writers, and other celebrities have been diagnosed with it. In recent years a number of celebrities and famous artists have publicly admitted that they suffer from bipolar disorder, including Catherine Zeta-Jones, Carrie Fisher, Linda Hamilton, and Jean-Claude Van Damme. There has also been speculation that many famous artists in the past were bipolar, too, such as Virginia Woolf, Edgar Allan Poe, and Vincent van Gogh.

Although cases such as these help increase awareness of the disorder, critics argue that in some cases it gives a false impression of bipolar disorder as always making people smart, creative, or otherwise worthy of fame. It is true that bipolar disorder does make some people extremely smart or creative and that they become famous as a result of their work. Yet in reality, for most people bipolar disorder is much more of a struggle than an asset. "There are plenty of geniuses who are not mentally ill, and there are plenty of mentally ill people who aren't geniuses," says Lloyd Sederer, medical director of the New York State Office of Mental Health. He points out that a combination of genius and bipolar disorder is actually relatively rare. Instead, he says, "One in four people annually in this country has a mental illness that impairs their function. That's pretty common. The illness is pervasive. Genius is much more rare."

Quoted in Sarah Klein, "What Neuroscience Has to Say About the 'Tortured Genius,'" *Huffington Post*, September 2, 2014. www.huffingtonpost.com.

A manic or hypomanic phase can be so enjoyable that many people are afraid to be treated for their illness, because they do not want to lose that feeling of pleasure and creativity. However, the highs of bipolar disorder can also cause harm. The National Alliance on Mental Illness warns, "A person may feel good while manic but may make choices that could seriously damage relationships, finances, health, home life or job prospects."[41]

Self-Injury and Suicide

No matter how enjoyable its highs can be, one of the most important reasons to treat bipolar disorder is the significant risk sufferers face for self-injury and suicide. The World Federation for Mental Health reports that 25 to 50 percent of people with bipolar disorder try to kill themselves at least once. A significant number of these attempts are successful. According to the Treatment Advocacy Center, about 15 percent of people with untreated bipolar disorder try to commit suicide; in comparison, the suicide rate for the general population is only about 1 percent.

It is believed that suicide is the number one cause of premature death among people with bipolar disorder. According to a 2014 report in *Scientific American*, suicide attempts are more common among women, though men are more likely to actually succeed in killing themselves. This seems to be due to the differences in the way that men and women generally attempt suicide; women are most likely to overdose on pills, which may not actually kill them, whereas men are more likely to use a firearm or hang themselves, which are more effective at causing death.

Bipolar patients who attempt suicide are usually not being treated, or their treatment is not effective. Suicide is usually due to extreme depression, a common symptom of the disorder. In a 2012 report in the *American Journal of Psychiatry*, researchers state that people are most likely to attempt suicide during a mixed episode. They explain, "Mixed states—depressive or manic—combine hopelessness with impulsivity and activation, leading to high risk for suicidal behavior."[42] In addition, the likelihood of suicide can increase when patients have psychotic symptoms, meaning that they lose touch with reality and may not fully understand the implications of their actions.

> "A person may feel good while manic but may make choices that could seriously damage relationships, finances, health, home life or job prospects."[41]
>
> —National Alliance on Mental Illness.

Bipolar Disorder and Violent Behavior

Although sufferers are far more likely to harm themselves, bipolar disorder sometimes does cause patients to act violently toward oth-

Younger Bipolar Patients Have More Emergency Room Visits

People with bipolar disorder sometimes have to visit the emergency room for complications related to their illness, such as psychosis or adverse reactions to medication. This graph shows the average number of emergency department visits made each year by bipolar patients of different ages. It reveals that patients aged fifteen to twenty-four are more likely to seek help at a hospital emergency room than other age groups.

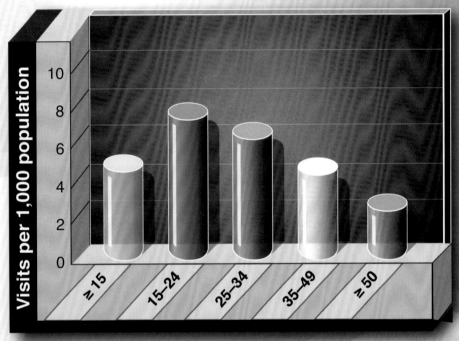

Source: Centers for Disease Control and Prevention, "QuickStats: Average Annual Rate of Emergency Department Visits for Bipolar Disorder Among Persons Aged ≥ 15 Years, by Age Group—National Hospital Ambulatory Medical Care Survey, United States, 2010–2011," *Morbidity and Mortality Weekly Report*, December 12, 2014. www.cdc.gov.

er people. As with suicide, this type of violence usually occurs when a patient is not being treated. For example, in 2013 twenty-four-year-old Gus Deeds of Virginia stabbed his father, Senator Creigh Deeds, multiple times in the face and body. Gus's sister Rebecca reported that her brother had been diagnosed with bipolar disorder three years earlier. She also said that right before the stabbing, their father had become concerned because Gus was agitated. He was worried that Gus was suicidal, so he got a court order to check him into a hospital for an evaluation. According to Rebecca, the stabbing occurred after Gus failed to receive treatment. She says, "Mental health workers could not locate a hospital bed, and Gus was sent home."[43] Creigh Deeds survived the attack, but Gus died after shooting himself.

Despite such incidents, violent behavior by people with bipolar disorder is actually rare and is generally exaggerated by the public. In 2013 researchers surveyed 1,530 US adults and found that almost half believed that people with a severe mental illness such as bipolar disorder are more dangerous than members of the general population. However, in reality, people with bipolar disorder are unlikely to be violent.

People with a serious mental illness (SMI) can be violent during episodes of psychosis, especially when they also have a substance abuse disorder. However, Thomas Insel, director of the NIMH, stresses that mental illness only causes a small amount of violence overall. As he writes, "Most people with SMI are *not* violent, and most violent acts are *not* committed by people with SMI. In fact, people with SMI are actually at higher risk of being victims of violence than perpetrators."[44] Insel points out that the most common type of violence that a person with SMI is likely to be involved in is violence against him- or herself in the form of suicide.

A Complicated Reality

Bipolar disorder is a complicated illness to live with and can harm people's lives in many ways. As a result, patients report that receiving a bipolar diagnosis can be very upsetting and difficult to come to terms with. Ruth C. White, an assistant professor of social work at Seattle University, says that even though she had worked with mentally ill people for years, it took a long time to get a handle on her own bipolar illness. In a book they coauthored, White and psychologist John D. Preston stress, "Finding out you have an incurable, chronic, serious mental illness is a difficult thing to deal with."[45]

Yet despite the often significant challenges, some people say they would be sad if their illness vanished, because there is value in some elements of it. As one woman named Sascha wrote about living with bipolar disorder: "Manic-depression is a sickness, a disease. But it's more complicated than that. . . . [It] lets [patients] see and feel things that other people can't; allows them to create art and music and words that grab people by the heart and soul—allows them to kiss the sky and come back down to tell the tale."[46]

CHAPTER 4

Can Bipolar Disorder Be Treated or Cured?

On a website about bipolar disorder, a woman calling herself "Gloria in Texas" posts that untreated bipolar disorder devastated her life when she was young. "My bipolar disorder showed up when I was in my teens," she writes. "By the time I was 18 I had quit school, left home, been raped, tried to commit suicide, was married and divorced and was using and selling drugs." However, since getting treatment, she has become what she considers a success story. "I take my meds every day, go to a bipolar support group every week, see my therapist every month and see my psychiatrist every quarter," she says. "I can hold down a job and have been married to the same man for 18 years. . . . For the most part I live a 'normal' life."[47]

There is no cure for bipolar disorder, and most people who have it will battle it for their whole life. However, Gloria's story and others like it show that bipolar disorder is treatable. Many sufferers report that their lives significantly improve after they begin treatment, which helps reduce the occurrence and severity of episodes and helps patients deal with their symptoms. Without treatment, bipolar disorder can worsen; episodes can occur more frequently and be more intense, behavior can become psychotic, and suicide can become a real possibility.

Medication

The majority of experts believe that medication is the most important treatment for bipolar disorder. Although doctors do not understand precisely how most bipolar medications work, they do know that these medications impact the function of various chemicals in the brain that help regulate a person's mood. Patients with bipolar disorder usually need to take medication for the rest of their lives; if they stop, their symptoms usually worsen. In treating bipolar disorder, doctors usually try a class of drugs called mood stabilizers first. Other commonly used medications are antidepressants, antipsychotics, antiseizure medication, and antianxiety drugs. Just as the symptoms of bipolar disorder are highly variable between individuals, so are the medications used to treat it. Many people take more than one medication and must try various combinations and dosages to find what works best for them.

Mood stabilizers help reduce the symptoms of both mania and depression, and they also help reduce the frequency of episodes. Lithium is the most common mood stabilizer prescribed for bipolar disorder. It is a naturally occurring salt and was the first drug approved by the US Food and Drug Administration (FDA) to treat bipolar disorder (it was approved in the 1970s). Although it does not work for everyone, lithium is very effective at reducing the duration, severity, and frequency of both manic and depressive episodes. Francis Mark Mondimore insists that for many people, lithium is a miracle drug. "Many . . . patients have taken lithium for decades with complete control of their illness," he says. "Some have been so stable that they haven't seen a psychiatrist in years."[48] In addition to lithium, a number of antiseizure medications are used as mood stabilizers in bipolar patients, including lamotrigine, valproate, and carbamazepine.

Antipsychotic medications are also commonly prescribed for bipolar patients. People with bipolar disorder sometimes lose touch with reality, experiencing delusions or hallucinations, and antipsychotic medications help reduce these symptoms. These medications also help calm manic patients, reducing their agitation and their racing thoughts and overactivity. Another benefit of antipsychotics is that they work very quickly, so they are often used to help calm a patient before slower-working medications such as lithium can take effect. Some people take antipsychotics only to reduce psychosis or agitation, whereas others actually use them as mood stabilizers, taking them on a regular basis to help maintain a stable mood.

The other type of medication commonly used to treat bipolar disorder is antidepressants. Antidepressants help prevent a person's

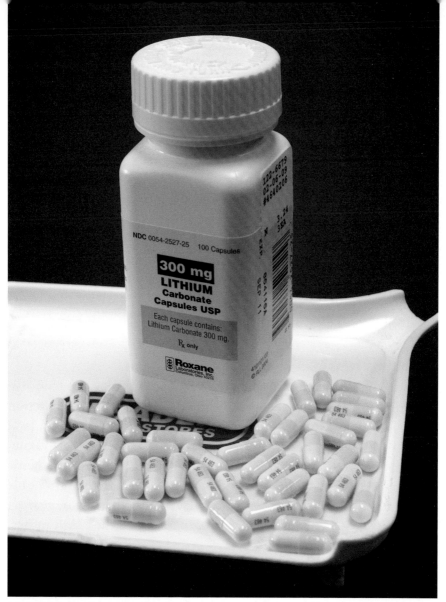

Lithium (pictured) is the most common mood stabilizer prescribed for bipolar disorder. A naturally occurring salt, it is generally effective at reducing the duration, severity, and frequency of manic and depressive episodes.

mood from plunging into depression. They are usually taken in combination with a mood stabilizing drug because there is evidence that if taken alone, they can actually cause mania or hypomania.

Scientists are also working to create new drugs with which to treat bipolar disorder. Many currently used bipolar drugs were discovered by chance or by trial and error. For example, the anticonvulsant valproate was originally approved by the FDA to treat epileptic seizures,

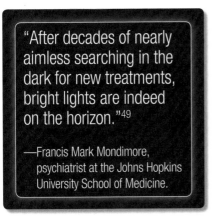

but doctors later discovered that it also helped some patients with bipolar disorder. Like valproate, a number of other medications used for bipolar disorder were originally used to treat other illnesses. As scientists gain an increasingly detailed understanding of the brain's chemistry, they are able to create drugs specifically designed for bipolar disorder. Mondimore reports that numerous new drugs are being developed: "After decades of nearly aimless searching in the dark for new treatments, bright lights are indeed on the horizon."[49]

Side Effects

Many of the medications used to treat bipolar disorder also have significant side effects. For instance, lithium can impair kidney function and cause hypothyroidism, a condition in which the thyroid gland does not function properly. Because of these risks, patients taking lithium must have regular blood tests to check their thyroid and kidney function. Overall, the list of potential side effects from various bipolar medications is long and includes dry mouth, diarrhea, constipation, heartburn, acne, drowsiness, dizziness, headaches, skin rashes, agitation, weight gain, and nausea.

Some of the drugs used to treat bipolar disorder pose extra risks for women and girls. Valproate can increase the levels of testosterone in a person's body, which in women can cause excess body hair, irregular menstrual cycles, and a condition called polycystic ovarian syndrome, which is a health problem that can affect fertility and pregnancy. Some medications pose a risk to a developing fetus and/or an infant, so pregnant women and nursing mothers must be cautious when taking bipolar medication.

In addition to these physical effects, some patients complain that their medication affects them mentally, too. Some bipolar patients say their medication takes away their creativity; others say they just do not feel like themselves. In a collection of writings about the disorder, a bipolar patient called "NG" describes this feeling, saying, "It's

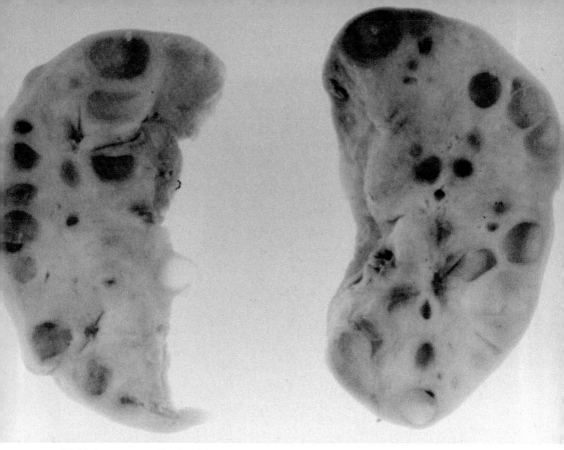

Multiple cysts are clearly visible on the ovaries of a woman with polycystic ovary syndrome. This syndrome is one possible side effect of a drug used to treat bipolar disorder.

seeing the machinery of my cognition be partially disassembled: certain wheels are spinning, but they aren't connected the way they were. . . . It's like I've taken the motor out or disconnected some belts and the motor is just spinning on its own. It's accompanied by a dullness and mild confusion."[50]

Finding the Right Combination

Many patients report that beginning new medication or changing medication is particularly difficult. Medication affects every patient differently, so patients often must try a number of different ones to find what works. In addition, a patient's needs may change over time, often necessitating a change in dosage or medication type. Bipolar patients consistently describe the discomfort associated with this process. For example, Peter Goodman suffers from bipolar disorder

Omega-3 Fatty Acids

Some researchers believe that omega-3 fatty acids, which are found in fish oils and some plant sources, may help reduce depressive symptoms in people with bipolar disorder. This idea came from the observation that some countries where people consume high levels of omega-3 fatty acids have lower rates of bipolar disorder. For instance, in 2011 researchers reported in the *Archives of General Psychiatry* that the lifetime incidence of bipolar disorder in Japan is less than 1 percent, compared to more than 4 percent in the United States. People in Japan eat a lot more fish than people in the United States, and fish contains omega-3 fatty acids.

Similarly, a 2012 article published in the *Journal of Clinical Psychology* reported that after reviewing five different studies about people with bipolar depression, researchers found strong evidence that omega-3 fatty acids improved bipolar depressive symptoms. Further research is needed on this topic, but researchers are optimistic about their findings so far. In addition, there are very few negative side effects from omega-3 fatty acids, and in most people none at all. Omega-3 fatty acids do not seem to have any effect on manic symptoms.

and says that taking the wrong medication can be even worse than taking none at all and that stopping a medicine can cause severe withdrawal symptoms similar to giving up heroin. He fears this condition more than anything. "I've spent weeks in utter misery as the psychiatrist tried different drugs on me to ease my depression or mania," he says. "In the interim I often found myself sitting in the bathtub with the shower trickling down on me, crying until I was hyperventilating, wishing I were dead."[51]

Going Without Medication

It is very common for people with bipolar disorder to stop taking their medication at some point. In some cases patients find the side effects too uncomfortable or distressing. In other cases patients stop taking their medication on purpose because episodes of mania or hypomania make them feel good, energetic, and productive, and they do not want to give that up.

Some people do not take medication, because they believe it is possible to successfully treat bipolar disorder without it. For example, *Forbes* contributor Michael Ellsberg says that he struggled with bipolar II for years, until he decided to follow the advice of a doctor who told him to stop eating refined sugar and drinking alcohol and coffee. Although Ellsberg was reluctant to give these up, he finally decided to challenge himself to go a year without them. "What came out of my year without sugar, coffee, or alcohol?" He says, "I got my life back." He says that it has been four years since he started the challenge, and he feels energized and in control of his life and no longer has mood swings. "I'm thirty-four, happy, and completely off all medications."[52] However, people such as Ellsberg are in the minority, and despite the negative side effects, it is generally accepted that medication is an important part of any treatment plan for an adult with bipolar disorder.

> "I've spent weeks in utter misery as the psychiatrist tried different drugs on me to ease my depression or mania."[51]
>
> —Peter Goodman, bipolar patient.

Medication for Children

Treating children with bipolar disorder medications is more controversial than treating adults. This is because there is very little research on the effects such medication will have on children. In fact, some of the medications used to treat bipolar disorder in adults have not been officially approved by the FDA for use in children. Instead, doctors prescribe these medications off-label, meaning that they are prescribing the medications for a use not approved by the FDA.

There is widespread disagreement over the impact of these drugs on children. Some argue that bipolar medications are powerful drugs with serious side effects that can harm children's developing brains and cause other serious health problems such as obesity and diabetes. Child psychiatrist Carrie Borchardt says that these powerful drugs actually cause some of the problems she sees in some of her young patients. "A substantial number of those kids, if you take them off the problem medication, those symptoms go away," she says. "And then they don't have bipolar, they just had a medication-induced problem."[53] Yet others insist that the problems caused by untreated bipolar disorder are worse than the risks from the medication.

Advocates of medicating children insist that identifying and treating bipolar disorder as early as possible can reduce the severity of the illness and the harm it inflicts on a child's life. "I understand the reason why a parent would be afraid to medicate their child. There are often serious and unknown side-effects to consider," says psychiatrist Janet Wozniak. "But parents also need to consider that there may be a downside to not medicating and missing an opportunity to interrupt the course of a serious illness. . . . Not medicating may also carry with it risks."[54] For example, one mother explains that her seven-year-old daughter is suicidal due to bipolar disorder. "Without treatment," she says, "I see my daughter as killing herself."[55]

Psychosocial Treatments

Although medication is an important part of treating bipolar disorder, psychosocial treatment is critical, too. Psychosocial treatment is a combination of therapy and education that teaches patients to understand and manage their disorder so it is less disruptive to their life. Research has shown that when patients undergo psychosocial treatments, they are more likely to recognize when they are experiencing symptoms and to address those symptoms so they experience fewer episodes as well as episodes of less severity. Psychosocial treatments include interpersonal and social rhythm therapy (IPSRT), cognitive behavioral therapy (CBT), family therapy, and group therapy.

Interpersonal and Social Rhythm Therapy

There is evidence that disturbances to a person's daily rhythms—such as his or her relationships, diet, or sleep—can trigger bipolar episodes. Thus, IPSRT is focused on developing a stable lifestyle with regular routines. There is a focus on keeping regular sleep routines and developing stable relationships with other people. Patients also learn to identify the major stresses and social issues that can interrupt their routines and to come up with a plan for addressing these disruptions when they occur.

Cognitive Behavioral Therapy

CBT is based on the idea that the way a person feels and behaves is a result of his or her thoughts. Therapists believe that certain types of negative thoughts cause negative feelings and behaviors for people with bipolar disorder. However, they also believe that people can change these negative feelings and behavior by changing their thoughts. In CBT bipolar patients learn how to monitor their thoughts and behavior. When they notice negative thoughts that are likely to worsen their symptoms, they learn how to replace these thoughts with positive ones. As a result of identifying and reducing negative feelings, patients have less-severe symptoms.

For instance, for people with bipolar disorder, stressful situations can cause negative feelings. This can be a trigger for a bipolar episode. CBT teaches people to change the negative feelings that they get from stress and thus reduce the chance of triggering an episode. A number of research studies have indicated that CBT is effective. Researchers have found that when people undergo CBT in addition to taking medication, they are likely to experience less-frequent and shorter episodes and are less likely to be hospitalized.

Family and Group Therapy

In addition to individual types of therapy such as IPSRT and CBT, many people with bipolar disorder benefit from family therapy. Bipolar disorder can wreak havoc on families because patients' symptoms are often difficult for others to deal with. That makes family life hard, and the increased stress can in turn worsen a patient's symptoms. In family therapy, family members attend sessions along with the patient. Therapists teach them to reduce the family stress and conflict that often occur as a consequence of bipolar disorder.

Group therapy involves a number of people with the same or similar problems, such as bipolar disorder or mood disorders. By engaging in group therapy, people with bipolar disorder learn about the experiences of others who face similar challenges. This can help them learn to deal better with their own challenges. Many patients also report that it is comforting to be around others who truly understand what it is like to live with bipolar disorder.

Recognizing Triggers

An important goal of all these types of therapy and education is to help patients recognize the early warning signs and triggers for mood episodes. If individuals notice early that their mood is starting to get too low or high, they can try to prevent more symptoms from developing or the episode from becoming more intense.

Common warning signs for mania or hypomania include sleeping less, having more energy, or feeling irritable. Warning signs for depression include feeling tired or enjoying normal activities less. Triggers can be good or bad things that happen in life and influence a person's mood. For example, losing a job could trigger depression, whereas getting a promotion could trigger mania. Therapists teach patients how to minimize their mood disturbance after recognizing the presence of early warning signs or triggers. For example, if individuals recognize signs of mania, they can practice self-calming activities such as getting more sleep or limiting the number of tasks they are doing. For depression, they can try to stay active and spend time with other people to keep their mood from getting worse. Although these may seem like commonsense activities, they are actually critical for bipolar people; if individuals start going into a manic or depressive mood, they must be very mindful about practicing these techniques.

Electroconvulsive Therapy

Sometimes, neither medication nor therapy is enough to stabilize a person's mood. In such cases people might turn to electroconvulsive therapy (ECT). This procedure involves passing an electric current through the brain. The current causes the brain to have a seizure, and this helps stabilize a person's mood by bringing the brain's electrical activity back to a more normal balance. In the 1950s and 1960s when ECT was a relatively new treatment, it was often unpleasant and in some cases actually harmful to patients. Authors Sarah Owen and Amanda Saunders explain that at that time, the treatment often

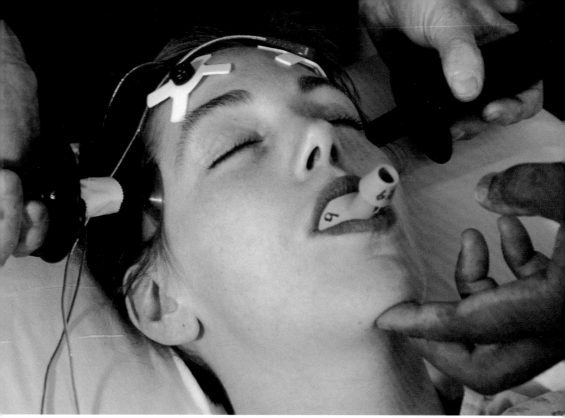

Doctors perform electroconvulsive therapy on a patient who suffers from depression. The act of passing an electric current through the brain can help stabilize mood by bringing balance to the brain's electrical activity.

caused significant discomfort and lasting problems. "Broken bones were not uncommon, as the electric currents could cause patients to thrash about, despite their restraints, and sometimes more than 100 ECT treatments could be administered to one person, causing severe memory loss and speech impairment."[56] In addition, ECT was often used on patients against their will.

ECT has greatly improved since then, however. It is far less traumatic than in the past. Doctors usually give patients a muscle relaxant to prevent them from thrashing about and a general anesthetic so they do not feel the electric current. Then an electrical impulse is administered, usually for thirty to ninety seconds. According to the NIMH, a person usually recovers from an ECT treatment in about five to fifteen minutes and is able to go home that same day. The NIMH adds that some of the short-term effects can include memory loss, confusion, and disorientation. According to bipolar experts Trisha Suppes and Ellen B. Dennehy, ECT can be very effective. They state, "The

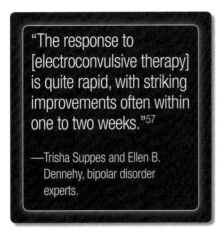

response to this treatment is quite rapid, with striking improvements often within one to two weeks."[57]

Yet despite great improvements in the procedure, ECT is usually reserved for cases in which patients are unable to take medication, such as women who are pregnant and do not want to risk harming a fetus with medication, or in cases in which medication and psychotherapy do not work.

Other Types of Brain Stimulation

Researchers are also investigating the effectiveness of other types of electrical stimulation. One is called transcranial magnetic stimulation (TMS). Unlike ECT, in which an electric current induces a seizure and anesthesia is necessary, the electric current in TMS is much smaller, with no anesthesia needed. In ECT, doctors apply an electric current to the scalp, and it goes into the brain. However, in TMS, no electricity actually passes through the skull. Instead, doctors hold a magnetic coil against the scalp, and its magnetic field causes a small electric current in the brain tissue underneath. Although there is some evidence that TMS helps bipolar patients, this treatment is still experimental, and additional research is needed on its effectiveness.

Another type of electrical stimulation is called vagal nerve stimulation (VNS). VNS has been shown to be effective in treating epilepsy, though researchers have recently begun to experiment with using it to treat depression in bipolar disorder. The vagus nerve runs from the base of the brain, down the neck, and into the chest and abdomen. For VNS, doctors surgically implant a small device that is similar to a pacemaker and constantly delivers electrical signals to the vagus nerve. Like TMS, VNS is still considered experimental.

Healthy Lifestyle Choices and Alternative Treatments

In addition to medication and therapy, many people with bipolar disorder find that making healthy lifestyle choices or using alternative

The Relief of Being Diagnosed

Many people report that a significant amount of relief comes simply from receiving a bipolar disorder diagnosis. Although being diagnosed can be upsetting because it confirms a person must face a lifetime of dealing with this difficult illness, some patients report it is also a positive experience. A diagnosis helps them understand why they have struggled with their moods and energy, and they no longer feel so confused about why they act and feel the way they do. For example, Elizabeth (not her real name), who had experienced symptoms since she was twelve or thirteen years old but was not diagnosed until she was twenty-four, says, "It was a really, really big relief when I found out. . . . It was just like a big light bulb went off in my head like, oh okay this explains everything. . . . I know what's going on now." Similarly, a woman named Alison says her daughter's diagnosis at age twelve was also a positive development. "It makes her feel as though she's not abnormal," says Alison. "She can think, 'I feel this way for a reason. . . . I'm not weird or freaky, this is just the way my body works.'"

Quoted in Regina Elizabeth Bates, "An Exploratory Study of the Experiences of Young Adults with Bipolar Disorder," master's thesis, California State University–Fresno, May 2014, p. 27.

Quoted in Sarah Owen and Amanda Saunders, *Bipolar Disorder—the Ultimate Guide*. Oxford: Oneworld, 2008, p. 44.

treatments helps reduce the severity of their illness. Healthy lifestyle choices include eating a healthy diet, not smoking or using recreational drugs, limiting alcohol and caffeine, exercising regularly, limiting stress, and getting enough sleep. For example, bipolar patient Elaina J. Martin says that she works hard to reduce stress in her life. She explains, "Unexpected stressors can lead to episodes for me so the better I can plan things, the more stable I am."[58] Some patients also try alternative treatments for bipolar disorder. These treatments include acupuncture, homeopathy, massage, meditation, yoga, and herbal remedies.

Medical professionals overwhelming agree that people with bipolar disorder must be treated, though individuals are different

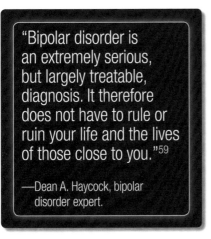

"Bipolar disorder is an extremely serious, but largely treatable, diagnosis. It therefore does not have to rule or ruin your life and the lives of those close to you."[59]

—Dean A. Haycock, bipolar disorder expert.

in the way they experience the illness. Thus, every patient is different in terms of what treatment works for him or her. In general, a combination of medication and therapy is the most common treatment, though the specifics are highly variable, particularly with medication. Overall, one of the most important things to understand is that in most cases bipolar disorder can be treated. As bipolar disorder expert Dean A. Haycock stresses, "Bipolar disorder is an extremely serious, but largely treatable, diagnosis. It therefore does not have to rule or ruin your life and the lives of those close to you."[59]

SOURCE NOTES

Introduction: A Bigger Problem than Most People Realize

1. Quoted in Sharon Cotilar, "Demi Lovato: I Have Bipolar Disorder," *People*, April 20, 2011. www.people.com.

2. Robert Grieco and Laura Edwards, *The Other Depression: Bipolar Disorder*. New York: Routledge, 2010, p. 2.

3. Quoted in Wayne Drash, "Mental Wellness Warriors: Fighting for Those Who Need It Most," CNN, January 17, 2015. www.cnn.com.

Chapter 1: What Is Bipolar Disorder?

4. Francis Mark Mondimore, *Bipolar Disorder: A Guide for Patients and Families*. Baltimore, MD: Johns Hopkins University Press, 2014, p. 8.

5. Quoted in Pat Hagan, "Manic Depression Has Been Rebranded as Bipolar . . . but Are So Many of Us Really Mentally Ill?," *Daily Mail* (London), April 18, 2011. www.dailymail.co.uk.

6. Steve Millard, *Bipolar Life: 50 Years of Battling Manic-Depressive Illness Did Not Stop Me from Building a 60 Million Dollar Business*. New York: Morgan James, 2011, pp. v–vi.

7. National Alliance on Mental Illness, "Criteria for a Manic Episode: DSM 5." www2.nami.org.

8. Quoted in Davey Alba, "How Smartphone Apps Can Treat Bipolar Disorder and Schizophrenia," *Wired*, November 20, 2014. www.wired.com.

9. Trisha Suppes and Ellen B. Dennehy, *Bipolar Disorder Assessment and Treatment*. Sudbury, MA: Jones & Bartlett Learning, 2012, p. 9.

10. Quoted in Sarah Owen and Amanda Saunders, *Bipolar Disorder— the Ultimate Guide*. Oxford: Oneworld, 2008, p. 25.

11. Quoted in Grieco and Edwards, *The Other Depression*, p. 14

12. National Alliance on Mental Illness, "Criteria for Major Depressive Episode: DSM-5." www2.nami.org.

13. Grieco and Edwards, *The Other Depression*, p. 34.

14. Depression and Bipolar Support Alliance, "Rapid Cycling and Its Treatment." www.dbsalliance.org.

15. Quoted in Owen and Saunders, *Bipolar Disorder—the Ultimate Guide*, pp. 29–30.

16. Owen and Saunders, *Bipolar Disorder—the Ultimate Guide*, p. 20.

17. Enrico Gnaulati, *Back to Normal: Why Ordinary Childhood Behavior Is Mistaken for ADHD, Bipolar Disorder, and Autism Spectrum Disorder*. Boston, MA: Beacon, 2013, p. 131.

18. Quoted in TeensHealth, "Bipolar Disorder," March 2012. http://kidshealth.org.

19. Mondimore, *Bipolar Disorder*, p. 1.

20. Mondimore, *Bipolar Disorder*, p. 1.

Chapter 2: What Causes Bipolar Disorder?

21. Gina Kolata, "5 Disorders Share Genetic Risk Factors, Study Finds," *New York Times*, February 28, 2013. www.nytimes.com.

22. William R. Marchand, *Depression and Bipolar Disorder: Your Guide to Recovery*. Boulder, CO: Bull, 2012, p. 89.

23. American Academy of Child & Adolescent Psychiatry, "Frequently Asked Questions: What Causes Pediatric Bipolar Disorder?," 2014. www.aacap.org.

24. American Academy of Child & Adolescent Psychiatry, "Frequently Asked Questions."

25. Quoted in Michele Hoos, "Back to School with Bipolar? How College Can Unleash Mania," CNN, September 21, 2010. www.cnn.com.

26. Quoted in Hoos, "Back to School with Bipolar? How College Can Unleash Mania."

27. Michelle, "Could a Concussion Have Triggered My Bipolar Disorder," HubPages, June 18, 2013. http://michellebell1972.hub pages.com.

28. Quoted in Tracy Pedersen, "Depression Often Turns to Bipolar Illness After Childbirth," Psych Central, November 10, 2013. http://psychcentral.com.

29. Quoted in Owen and Saunders, *Bipolar Disorder—the Ultimate Guide*, p. 40.

Chapter 3: What Is It like to Live with Bipolar Disorder?

30. Peter Goodman, *Buzzkill: One Man's Struggle with Bipolar Disorder*. Charleston, SC: CreateSpace, 2011, pp. 13–14.

31. Quoted in Mondimore, *Bipolar Disorder*, p. 176.

32. Owen and Saunders, *Bipolar Disorder—the Ultimate Guide*, p. 2.

33. CJ Laymon, "Why I Keep My Bipolar Disorder Secret at Work," *Atlantic*, August 22, 2013. www.theatlantic.com.

34. Lorna Evans, "Two For: Memories of a Manic Father," Psych Central, 2014. http://psychcentral.com.

35. Igor Galynker and Jessica Briggs, "Expert Commentary: 'Hidden' Bipolar Disorder Patients," *Internal Medicine News*, August 1, 2013. www.imng.com.

36. Natasha Tracy, "Keeping a Job When You Have Bipolar Disorder," HealthyPlace, September 3, 2013. www.healthyplace.com.

37. Sarah Freeman, "My Bipolar Disorder Wrecked My Finances," *Credit.com* (blog), June 19, 2013. http://blog.credit.com.

38. National Alliance on Mental Illness, "The Impact and Cost of Mental Illness: The Case of Bipolar Disorder," 2015. www2.nami .org.

39. Quoted in Owen and Saunders, *Bipolar Disorder—the Ultimate Guide*, p. 243.

40. Quoted in Owen and Saunders, *Bipolar Disorder—the Ultimate Guide*, p. xvii.

41. National Alliance on Mental Illness, "What Is Bipolar Disorder?" www.nami.org.

42. Alan C. Swann et al., "Bipolar Mixed States: An International Society for Bipolar Disorders Task Force Report of Symptom Structure, Course of Illness, and Diagnosis," *American Journal of Psychiatry*, January 2013. http://ajp.psychiatryonline.org.

43. Rebecca Deeds, "What the World Needs to Know About My Brother," *Glamour*, September 2014. www.glamour.com.

44. Thomas Insel, "Understanding Severe Mental Illness," *Director's Blog*, National Institute of Mental Health, January 11, 2013. www.nimh.nih.gov.

45. Ruth C. White and John D. Preston, *Bipolar 101: A Practical Guide to Identifying Triggers, Managing Medications, Coping with Symptoms, and More*. Oakland, CA: New Harbinger, 2009, p. 1.

46. Quoted in Icarus Project, *Navigating the Space Between Brilliance and Madness: A Reader and Roadmap of Bipolar Worlds*. Oakland, CA: AK, 2013, p. 22.

Chapter 4: Can Bipolar Disorder Be Treated or Cured?

47. Gloria in Texas, comment on Curt in Altoona, "A Bipolar Disorder Success Story," Bipolar Happens, January 12, 2013. http://bipolarhappens.com.

48. Mondimore, *Bipolar Disorder*, p. 83.

49. Mondimore, *Bipolar Disorder*, p. 97.

50. Quoted in Icarus Project, *Navigating the Space Between Brilliance and Madness*, p. 63.

51. Goodman, *Buzzkill*, p. 11.

52. Michael Ellsberg, "How I Overcame Bipolar II (and Saved My Own Life)," *Forbes*, July 18, 2011. www.forbes.com.

53. Quoted in Jeremy Olson, "Bipolar Label Soars Among Kids," *Minneapolis (MN) Star Tribune*, June 23, 2011. www.startribune .com.

54. Quoted in Korina Lopez, "Parents Struggle with Decision to Medicate Bipolar Kids," *USA Today*, December 8, 2012. www .usatoday.com.

55. Quoted in Lopez, "Parents Struggle with Decision to Medicate Bipolar Kids."

56. Owen and Saunders, *Bipolar Disorder—the Ultimate Guide*, p. 20.

57. Suppes and Dennehy, *Bipolar Disorder Assessment and Treatment*, pp. 51, 53.

58. Quoted in Margarita Tartakovsky, "Building a Routine When You Have Bipolar Disorder," Psych Central, 2014. http://psych central.com.

59. Dean A. Haycock, *The Everything Health Guide to Adult Bipolar Disorder*. Avon, MA: Adams Media, 2010, p. 251.

ORGANIZATIONS TO CONTACT

American Academy of Child & Adolescent Psychiatry (AACAP)
3615 Wisconsin Ave. NW
Washington, DC 20016
phone: (202) 966-7300
fax: (202) 966-2891
website: www.aacap.org

The AACAP is the leading national professional medical association dedicated to treating and improving the quality of life for children, adolescents, and families affected by mental, behavioral, or developmental disorders, including bipolar disorder. The AACAP distributes information in an effort to promote an understanding of mental illnesses and remove the stigma associated with them, advance efforts in prevention of mental illnesses, and assure proper treatment and access to services for children and adolescents.

American Psychiatric Association (APA)
1000 Wilson Blvd., Suite 1825
Arlington, VA 22209
phone: (703) 907-7300
e-mail: apa@psych.org
website: www.psych.org

The APA is the world's largest professional psychiatric organization and works to provide effective treatment for people with mental disorders. Its website provides information about bipolar disorder.

Brain & Behavior Research Foundation
90 Park Ave., 16th Floor
New York, NY 10016
phone: (646) 681-4888
e-mail: info@bbrfoundation.org
website: https://bbrfoundation.org

The Brain & Behavior Research Foundation works to reduce the suffering caused by mental illness. It awards grants for research on bipolar disorder and other types of mental illness. The organization's website has information about bipolar disorder, including recent research findings, and stories from people who live with the disorder.

Depression and Bipolar Support Alliance (DBSA)
55 E. Jackson Blvd., Suite 490
Chicago, IL 60604
phone: (800) 826-3632
fax: (312) 642-7243
website: www.dbsalliance.org

The DBSA works to provide support and education that will improve the lives of people who have mood disorders, including bipolar disorder. Its website provides statistics about bipolar disorder and information about the treatment of this illness.

Mental Health America (MHA)
2000 N. Beauregard St., 6th Floor
Alexandria, VA 22311
phone: (703) 684-7722
fax: (703) 684-5968
website: www.nmha.org

The MHA is a nonprofit organization dedicated to helping all people live mentally healthier lives. It works to help people understand how to protect and improve their mental health and when to look for help for themselves or friends or family members. The MHA's website contains numerous fact sheets on bipolar disorder.

National Alliance on Mental Illness (NAMI)
Colonial Place Three
2107 Wilson Blvd., Suite 300
Arlington, VA 22201
phone: (703) 524-7600
fax: (703) 524-9094
e-mail: info@nami.org
website: www.nami.org

The NAMI is an organization dedicated to eradicating mental illness and improving the quality of life for all people affected by mental illness. It provides support, education, and advocacy for those affected by bipolar disorder. Its website provides research and fact sheets about this disorder and the medications used to treat it.

National Institute of Mental Health (NIMH)

6001 Executive Blvd.
Rockville, MD 20852
phone: (301) 443-4513
fax: (301) 443-4279
e-mail: nimhinfo@nih.gov
website: www.nimh.nih.gov

The NIMH is dedicated to research that will reduce the burden of mental illness and behavioral disorders, including bipolar disorder. Its website contains fact sheets, overviews, and recent research updates on the disorder.

Treatment Advocacy Center

200 N. Glebe Rd., Suite 801
Arlington, VA 22203
phone: (703) 294-6001
fax: (703) 294-6010
e-mail: info@treatmentadvocacycenter.org
website: www.treatmentadvocacycenter.org

The Treatment Advocacy Center is a national nonprofit organization that works to reform treatment of severe mental illnesses, including bipolar disorder. Its website contains a number of reports and blog entries about the treatment of bipolar disorder.

FOR FURTHER RESEARCH

Books

Janelle M. Caponigro et al., *Bipolar Disorder: A Guide for the Newly Diagnosed*. Oakland, CA: New Harbinger, 2012.

Robert Grieco and Laura Edwards, *The Other Depression: Bipolar Disorder*. New York: Routledge, 2010.

Dean A. Haycock, *The Everything Health Guide to Adult Bipolar Disorder*. Avon, MA: Adams Media, 2010.

Francis Mark Mondimore, *Bipolar Disorder: A Guide for Patients and Families*. Baltimore, MD: Johns Hopkins University Press, 2014.

Trisha Suppes and Ellen B. Dennehy, *Bipolar Disorder Assessment and Treatment*. Sudbury, MA: Jones & Bartlett Learning, 2012.

Eduard Vieta, *Managing Bipolar Disorder in Clinical Practice*. London: Springer, 2013.

Internet Sources

Michael Ellsberg, "How I Overcame Bipolar II (and Saved My Own Life)," *Forbes*, July 18, 2011. www.forbes.com/sites/michaelellsberg/2011/07/18/how-i-overcame-bipolar-ii.

Sarah Klein, "What Neuroscience Has to Say About the 'Tortured Genius,'" *Huffington Post*, September 2, 2014. www.huffingtonpost.com/2014/09/02/creativity-mental-illness-health_n_5695887.html.

CJ Laymon, "Why I Keep My Bipolar Disorder Secret at Work," *Atlantic*, August 22, 2013. www.theatlantic.com/health/archive/2013/08/why-i-keep-my-bipolar-disorder-secret-at-work/278931.

Korina Lopez, "Parents Struggle with Decision to Medicate Bipolar Kids," *USA Today*, December 8, 2012. www.usatoday.com/story/news/nation/2012/12/07/bipolar-kids-parents-medication/1754931.

National Institute of Mental Health, "Bipolar Disorder in Adults," 2012. www.nimh.nih.gov/health/publications/bipolar-disorder-in-adults/index.shtml?rf=.

Treatment Advocacy Center, "Bipolar Disorder—Fact Sheet," 2011. www.treatmentadvocacycenter.org/resources/briefing-papers-and-fact-sheets/159/463.

Websites

Bipolar World (www.bipolarworld.net). This website offers information about bipolar disorder, as well as chat rooms where people affected by the disorder can share their experiences and support one another.

International Bipolar Foundation (http://ibpf.org). This website provides information and support for bipolar patients and for friends and family of those with the disorder.

INDEX

Note: Boldface page numbers indicate illustrations.

Abbott, Paul, 45
abuse, as factor in bipolar
   disorder, 33–34
American Academy of Child
   & Adolescent Psychiatry
   (AACAP), 30–31, 38–39
American Journal of Psychiatry,
   34, 47
American Psychiatric
   Association, 11
antidepressants, 27, 52–53
Archives of General Psychiatry
   (journal), 8, 20, 38, 56

baby blues (postpartum
   depression), 34
Bates, Regina Elizabeth, 43
bipolar disorder
   abuse as factor in, 33
   basic types of, 18–19
   brain structure/function
      and, 29–30
   in children, 22–23
   creative occupations and,
      45–46
   emergency room visits
      among people with, by age
      group, 48
   environmental factors in,
      30–32
   financial impact of, 43–44

following head injury, 33–34
genetic factors in, 25–28
health conditions coexisting
   with, 38
hormonal changes and,
   34–35
mixed episodes/rapid
   cycling in, 16–17
prevalence of, 6, 20
relationships and, 41–42
risk factors for, 20, 21, 22
   reducing, 35–36
social stigma and, 40–41
untreated, 9
violent behavior and, 47–49
work/school and, 42–43
See also diagnosis;
   treatment(s)
Bipolar Disorders (journal), 34
brain
   structure and function, in
      bipolar disorder, 29–30
   trauma to, 33–34
Briggs, Jessica, 42

childbirth, 34–35
children
   bipolar disorder in, 22–23
   medication for, 57–58
Clinical Psychology Review
   (journal), 33
cognitive behavioral therapy
   (CBT), 59
Craddock, Nick, 35–36

cyclothymia, 19
cystic fibrosis, inheritance of, 28, **29**

Deeds, Creigh, 48, 49
Deeds, Gus, 48–49
Deeds, Rebecca, 48–49
Dennehy, Ellen B., 14, 61–62
depression, 10
    symptoms of, 14
    warning signs for episodes of, 60
Depression and Bipolar Support Alliance, 7, 17, 26
diagnosis
    of depression, criteria for, 14–15
    difficulty with, 8, 38
    of mania, criteria for, 13
    relief from, 63
Diagnostic and Statistical Manual of Mental Disorders (DSM), 8, 13

electroconvulsive therapy (ECT), 60–62, **61**
Ellsberg, Michael, 57
emergency room visits, among people with bipolar disorder, **48**
environment, as factor in bipolar disorder, 30–32
Evans, Lorna, 41–42

family therapy, 59–60
Federman, Russell, 32, 33

Food and Drug Administration, US (FDA), 27, 57
Freeman, Sarah, 43–44

Galynker, Igor, 42
gender differences, 22
genes, 27–28
genetics, 25–29
Gnaulati, Enrico, 23
Goodman, Peter, 37, 55–56, 57
Grieco, Robert, 8, 9, 40
group therapy, 59–60

Haycock, Dean A., 64
hypomania, 14

Insel, Thomas, 49
interpersonal and social rhythm therapy (IPSRT), 58–59

Journal of Clinical Psychiatry, 38
Journal of Clinical Psychology, 56
Journal of Psychiatric Research, 45
Journal of Psychiatry & Neuroscience, 25
Juvenile Bipolar Research Foundation, 23

Kolata, Gina, 29
Kraepelin, Emil, 11

lithium, 52, 53
Lovato, Demi, 6, 7, 9

mania, 10, 11, 13
   likelihood of symptoms of,
      12
   productivity and, 45–46
   warning signs for episodes
      of, 60
manic-depressive illness, 11
Marchand, William R., 30
Martin, Elaina J., 63
McClure, Kristen, 22
mental illness
   genetic component of,
      28–29
   prevalence of, 20, 21
   violence and, 49
Mental Illness Policy Org., 38
Millard, Steve, 11
mixed episodes, 16–17
Mondimore, Francis Mark,
   10, 23–24, 40, 52, 54
mood disorders, 10
mood stabilizers, 52

National Alliance on Mental
   Illness, 6, 46, 47
National Institute of Mental
   Health (NIMH), 20, 22, 23,
   30
   on electroconvulsive
      therapy, 61
   on health disorders
      coexisting with bipolar
      disorders, 38
   on rapid cycling, 17

neurotransmitters, 30

omega-3 fatty acids, 56
Owen, Sarah, 19, 41, 60–61

polycystic ovary syndrome,
   54, 55
postpartum depression (baby
   blues), 34
prefrontal cortex, 30
Preston, John D., 49
Psychiatric Genomics
   Consortium (PGC), 28
psychosis, 17–18
   violence and, 49

rapid cycling, 16–17
risk factors, 20, 21, 22
   reducing, 35–36

Saunders, Amanda, 19, 41,
   60–61
Scientific American
   (magazine), 47
Sederer, Lloyd, 46
Shanahan, William, 11
sleep disturbances, 40
substance abuse, 35, 38–40
suicide, 46–47
   mixed episodes and, 17
Suppes, Trisha, 61–62
symptoms
   of bipolar depression, 15
   manic, 13
      likelihood of, 12

Timlin, Bryan, 13

Tracy, Natasha, 43
transcranial magnetic
  stimulation (TMS), 62
treatment(s)
  alternative, 62–64
  brain stimulation, 62
  cognitive behavioral therapy,
    59
  electroconvulsive therapy,
    60–62, 61
  family/group therapy, 59–60
  interpersonal and social
    rhythm therapy, 58–59
  lack of, for people with
    symptoms, 7–8
  medication, 51–54
    in children, 57–58

patients' compliance with,
    56–57
  side effects of, 54–55
  patients' recognition of triggers
    as goal of, 60

vagal nerve stimulation (VNS),
    62
valproate, 53–54
Vieta, Eduard, 37

White, Ruth C., 49
World Federation for Mental
  Health, 47
World Health Organization
  (WHO), 9, 20
Wozniak, Janet, 58

PICTURE CREDITS

ABOUT THE AUTHOR

Andrea C. Nakaya, a native of New Zealand, holds a BA in English and an MA in communications from San Diego State University. She has written and edited more than thirty-five books on current issues. She currently lives in Encinitas, California, with her husband and their two children, Natalie and Shane.